J. Laurence (James Laurence) Laughlin

The Study of Political Economy

Hints to Students and Teachers

J. Laurence (James Laurence) Laughlin

The Study of Political Economy
Hints to Students and Teachers

ISBN/EAN: 9783337073237

Printed in Europe, USA, Canada, Australia, Japan

Cover: Foto ©Suzi / pixelio.de

More available books at **www.hansebooks.com**

THE STUDY

OF

POLITICAL ECONOMY.

HINTS TO STUDENTS AND TEACHERS.

BY

J. LAURENCE LAUGHLIN, Ph. D.,

ASSISTANT PROFESSOR OF POLITICAL ECONOMY IN HARVARD UNIVERSITY.

NEW YORK ·:· CINCINNATI ·:· CHICAGO

AMERICAN BOOK COMPANY.

FROM THE PRESS OF
D. APPLETON & COMPANY.

FILIUS

MATRI BENIGNÆ.

PREFACE.

THE existence of this little book is due to an attempt to convey, by lectures to students, an understanding of the position which political economy holds in regard, not merely to its actual usefulness for every citizen, but to its disciplinary power, and to the qualities of mind which are necessary for success in the study. It was hoped, thereby, that young men might more intelligently decide whether they should begin the study, and, even when they had pur-sued it for a time, whether they should continue it. Each man by his own judgment, after an analysis such as is given within of the powers required for the study of political economy, should be enabled to come to a decision for himself more wisely than any one else could reach it for him. I desired in this way to aid

in a judicious selection of courses by the student who had some freedom of choice in his
college course.

The interest which the public now manifests
in economic studies led me to put the material
of my lectures into a general form, in order that
they might assist inquirers in any part of the
country. No special knowledge has, therefore,
been demanded of the reader by way of preparation for the substance of what I have introduced into this volume. By avoiding, as far as
possible, all technical language, I have sought
to make the inquiry useful to any general reader of intelligence who may be interested to
know how to study political economy. But
that which I have most at heart is the extension of instruction in political economy in all
schools and colleges, and the improvement in
methods of teaching the subject. I need hardly
say that I shall be glad if these pages call out
any suggestions by which these two objects
may be furthered.

J. LAURENCE LAUGHLIN.

HARVARD UNIVERSITY,
CAMBRIDGE, MASS., *May,* 1885.

CONTENTS.

―――――

CHAPTER I.

CHAPTER II.

CHAPTER III.

CHAPTER IV.

CHAPTER V.

A TEACHER'S LIBRARY,

ENGLISH, FRENCH, AND GERMAN AUTHORS.

GENERAL TREATISES.

John Stuart Mill's "Principles of Political Economy." Abridged, with critical, bibliographical, and explanatory notes, and a sketch of the History of Political Economy, by J. Laurence Laughlin. A text-book for colleges (1884).

Professor Fawcett's " Manual of Political Economy" (London, sixth edition, 1883) is a brief statement of Mill's book, with additional matter on the precious metals, slavery, trades-unions, co-operation, local taxation, etc.

Antoine-Élise Cherbuliez's " Précis de la science économique" (Paris, 1862, 2 vols.) follows the same arrangement as Mill, and is considered the best treatise on economic science in the French language. He is methodical, profound, and clear, and separates pure from applied political economy.

Other excellent books in French are: Courcelle-Seneuil's "Traité théorique et pratique d'économie politique" (1858), (Paris, second edition, 1867, 2 vols.), and a compendium by Henri Baudrillart, " Manuel d'économie politique" (third edition, 1872).

Roscher's "Principles of Political Economy" is a good example of the German historical method : its notes are crowded with facts ; but the English translation (New York, 1878) is badly done. There is an excellent translation of it into French by Wolowski.

A desirable elementary work, "The Economics of Industry" (London, 1879; second edition, 1881), was prepared by Mr. and Mrs. Marshall.

Professor Jevons wrote a "Primer of Political Economy" (1878), which is a simple, bird's-eye view of the subject in a very narrow compass.

IMPORTANT GENERAL WORKS.

Adam Smith's "Wealth of Nations" (1776). The edition of McCulloch is perhaps more serviceable than that of J. E. T. Rogers.

Ricardo's "Principles of Political Economy and Taxation" (1817).

J. S. Mill's "Principles of Political Economy" (2 vols., 1848—sixth edition, 1865).

Schönberg's "Handbuch der politischen Oekonomie" (1882). This is a large co-operative treatise by twenty-one writers from the historical school.

Cairnes's "Leading Principles of Political Economy" (1874); "Logical Method" (1875), lectures first delivered in Dublin in 1857.

Carey's "Social Science" (1877). This has been abridged in one volume by Kate McKean.

F. A. Walker's "Political Economy" (1883). This author differs from other economists, particularly on wages and questions of distribution.

TREATISES ON SPECIAL SUBJECTS.

W. T. Thornton's "On Labor" (1869).

H. George's "Progress and Poverty" (1879). In connection with this, read F. A. Walker's "Land and Rent" (1884).

J. Caird's "Landed Interest" (fourth edition, 1880), treating of English land and the food-supply.

McLeod's "Theory and Practice of Banking" (second edition, 1875-1876).

Goschen's "Theory of Foreign Exchanges" (eighth edition, 1875).

W. G. Sumner's "History of American Currency" (1874).

John Jay Knox's "United States Notes " (1884).

Jevons's "Money and the Mechanism of Exchange" (1875).

Tooke and Newmarch's "History of Prices" (1837–1856), in six volumes.

M. Block's "Traité théorique et pratique de statistique" (1878).

Leroy-Beaulieu's "Traité de la science des finances" (1883). This is an extended work, in two volumes, on taxation and finance; "Essai sur la répartition des richesses" (second edition, 1883).

F. A. Walker's "The Wages Question" (1876); "Money" (1878).

L. Reybaud's "Études sur les réformateurs contemporains, ou socialistes modernes " (seventh edition, 1864).

Rae's "Contemporary Socialism" (1884) gives a compendious statement of the tenets of modern socialists. See, also, R. T. Ely's "French and German Socialism" (1883).

DICTIONARIES.

McCulloch's "Commercial Dictionary" (new and enlarged edition, 1882).

Lalor's "Cyclopædia of Political Science" (1881–1884) is devoted to articles on political science, political economy, and American history.

Coquelin and Guillaumin's "Dictionnaire de l'économie politique" (1851–1853, third edition, 1864), in two large volumes.

REPORTS AND STATISTICS.

The "Compendiums of the Census" for 1840, 1850, 1860, and 1870, are desirable. The volumes of the tenth census

(1880) are of great value for all questions; as is also F. A. Walker's "Statistical Atlas" (1874); and Scribner's "Statistical Atlas of the United States," based on the census of 1880.

The United States Bureau of Statistics issues quarterly statements; and annually a report on "Commerce and Navigation," and another on the "Internal Commerce of the United States."

The "Statistical Abstract" is an annual publication, by the same department, compact and useful. It dates only from 1878.

The Director of the Mint issues an annual report dealing with the precious metals and the circulation. Its tables are important.

The Comptroller of the Currency (especially during the administration of J. J. Knox) has given important annual reports upon the banking systems of the United States.

The reports of the Secretary of the Treasury deal with the general finances of the United States. These, with the two last mentioned, are bound together in the volume of "Finance Reports," but often shorn of their tables.

There are valuable special reports to Congress of commissioners on the tariff, shipping, and other subjects, published by the Government.

The report on the "International Monetary Conference of 1878" contains a vast quantity of material on monetary questions.

The British parliamentary documents contain several annual "Statistical Abstracts" of the greatest value, of which the one relating to other European states is peculiarly convenient and useful. These can always be purchased at given prices.

A. R. Spofford's "American Almanac" is an annual of great usefulness.

J. H. Hickcox, Washington, publishes a very useful monthly catalogue of the Government publications, entitled "United States Publications."

CHAPTER I.

OUR CIVIL WAR THE CAUSE OF A NEW INTEREST IN ECONOMICS.

IN some parts of our country there is a current maxim among the old-fashioned gardeners, to the effect that "a wind-shaken tree will bear the more fruit." By widening its application, we shall find in it no little subtle force. In fact, it is a homely expression of an idea which undoubtedly finds its parallel in individual and social life. As individuals, we all know that there is no real growth of character except by a conquest over opposing difficulties; to do right when it is against our inclinations and prejudices strengthens the moral fiber, so that the firm organism gives forth fairer and sweeter fruit. But carry the analogy one step farther —from the individual to society. In the social organism it is possible that we may find, as it were, a moral law of conservation of energy, by

2

which there appears a relation between a loss
and a gain; so that a sacrifice becomes the parent of a subsequent good. Some great convul-
sions in political life find their justification when
viewed in the light of this truth, and by it history often reveals to us some different lessons
than those which lie on the surface of events;
but it is the most natural thing that this interpretation should escape the minds of the partici-
pants in the sacrifice, because the future gain
may lie at such a distance and be so impalpable
as even to elude considerable foresight. We
are, however, already reaching that interesting
distance from the events of the civil war where
we can begin to study them historically, and to
consider some of their evident effects. A few
years ago, we saw armies go out of our sight
during the civil war, only to come back thinned,
injured by disease, with half their number left
dead on the field. Death meant bitter, inde-
scribable sorrow in all our homes. The experiences of the war were felt to be pitiless, inex-
plicable, and hard. And yet, perhaps, a subtle
suggestion may have passed into some of our
minds that it was not simply by dying, or in

living, that the best law of our being was en-
forced ; that there was, in truth, some Power behind it all; that some purpose was being worked
out through each one of us; and that, although
not comprehended by us all, each one was as
necessary to the whole in the same way, for
example, that each leaf is necessary to the com-
pleted organism of the whole tree, and ceases to
be when it is separated from the stem.   But yet
it may be possible, without presuming too much,
to begin to look for some of the results of that
social and political upheaval which we must
now admit has been the greatest and most considerable disturbance in our national life since
the foundation of the government.   It is worth
while to examine whether the wind-shaken tree
has borne the more fruit.

The process by which citizens from secluded
districts and remote towns were sent through
new cities to opposite parts of the Union, ex-
changing ideas with men of different habits of
thought, was a marked feature of the war period,
and leavened the mental life of the American
people in a way hitherto little suspected.   It
was something like sending a country boy to

college, where he changes the ideas of the farm
for what is best in literature and science ; but, in
the case of the war, it was a college of national
politics and struggles, and, instead of one boy,
there were a million men.   The rural population came into a knowledge of our cities, while
the urban classes were carried away into new
climates, and into unvisited parts of our vast
domain.   New sights, new methods of cultivation, different standards of living, stimulated the
dull and fired the active and enterprising men
in the ranks.   The life of the farm and the vil-
lage was widened to an interest in the nation.
About the same time, moreover, the vast increase in easy means of communication by railways, and a great extension of the use of the newspaper and telegraph, which were stimulated by
the war exigencies, brought provincial towns into
direct connection with the outside world.   In
the process of comparison with the more attractive habits of the dwellers in the great cities and
towns, even oddities of customs and dress began
to disappear.   In various ways like this, the
thinking horizon was extended.   The presence
of complicated problems dawned upon the con-

sciousness of dull intellects, and brighter minds found new spurs to ambition in the questions of larger interest. On all sides men felt themselves coming into contact daily with new difficulties, under a dim comprehension of their bigness, but with a strong belief that their knowledge of how to deal with them was inadequate. In short, the tremendous crisis through which we passed during our civil war, apart from its effect on the preservation of the Union, has had a wide, although subtle, influence on the moral and intellectual character of the American people.

It can easily be imagined that the working of these new forces should have had a serious effect on a quick and susceptible race. Under somewhat similar conditions, they have, in fact, had a distinct influence on a more phlegmatic people than our own. Old students at Göttingen, on returning to the university since the late wars in which Germany has been engaged, are amazed to find the old-fashioned spot —where the customs, habits, and naïve simplicity of one hundred years ago had prevailed until quite recently—now wholly changed. The com-

mercial spirit has seized the formerly simple-
minded peasants, and the quiet town now hears
in its streets the heavy march of cosmopolitan-
ism.

The United States, as well as Germany, had
new problems to solve. The conflict of arms
ended the long slavery struggle, it is true, but
the war brought with it intricate questions of a
character very different from those which had
gone before. Without warning, and consequently without the opportunity to make due
preparation or acquire proper training, our public men were confronted, as the war progressed,
with matters of vital importance not only in international and constitutional law, but in taxation,
and in every form of administration and finance.
The demand for men who had devoted themselves
earnestly to the study of governmental science
was an imperative one; but, generally speaking,
it was met in a way which showed that there
existed in the community a class from whom
these necessary men could be recruited. That
class was the legal profession of the country.
The questions of reconstruction, the relation of
the Federal Government to the States, the civil

rights of the negro, our attitude toward foreign powers during the blockade of the Southern ports, were not abandoned to men who had never habituated themselves to discussions such as were involved in their settlement. There were differences of opinion, of course; but, inasmuch as these differences of opinion were the outcome of different political theories, this itself proved that attention had been previously given to such subjects to the extent that crystallized systems of thought, formulated in dogmas, had been created by the various parties. It may then be truly said that, in respect of political questions, we were not wholly unprepared for the emergencies of the war.

But, as has been suggested, other considerations than those of a legal and constitutional character arose, and new burdens were laid upon the public men of that day. The magnitude of the military operations involved an expenditure of money by the State on so large a scale as to demand from our statesmen a financial skill of an almost unparalleled kind. To meet these newly-presented questions of taxation finance, and currency, upon what body of men could we call? To this, answer must be frankly made that the war overtook us without a supply of, or even a few, trained economists and financiers in public life. The economic part in the equipment of a public official had been hitherto almost wholly neglected. In fact, political economy and finance had never been seriously studied in the schools; but, if studied at all, they had been classed in the old-fashioned required curriculum with Butler's " Analogy " and the " Evidences of Christianity." They had been, moreover, compressed into the briefest possible time, which would naturally assure, if not a dislike of the study, at least a superficiality even worse than total ignorance. Although Adam Smith wrote his " Wealth of Nations " in 1776, it is a mortifying fact that political economy was practically an unknown science to the American people before 1860.

When this fact is considered, and when we realize how unfit we were to handle economic problems skillfully, it is an interesting study to look into the way in which our people took up the burdens and tasks of our great civil conflict. There was the quick adaptability of

Americans to start with; there was plenty of patriotism and good-will, and no lack of those high qualities of self-sacrifice and heroism which are still fragrant to us; but lawyers, such as Chase and Fessenden, were practically our only financiers. Operations which required patience, experience, knowledge, and leadership had to be carried on by men who had no such qualities. Early in the war they were required to consider a scheme of raising loans, and to adjust a plan of taxation corresponding to the extraordinary war expenses; but the banks became loaded with unsalable United States bonds, and, unguided, the country drifted at once into a position where specie payments were suspended at the end of 1861. Without considering alternatives, they created a national debt in a few years as great as that incurred by old despotisms of Europe in centuries; without foresight, or financial leadership, they fell into a ruinous issue of irredeemable paper money, which even yet, although somewhat contracted, still remains a source of anxiety and danger; without intending it as the aim of a definite policy, but simply through a desire to gain a war revenue, they imposed heavy customs duties on imports, which have brought into existence business interests largely dependent on the continuance of these temporary war-measures. When it is realized that principles of taxation are probably less understood to-day, even by intelligent men, than any other branch of economics, it is not surprising to find that in 1864 Congress was occupied only five days in passing through both its branches the most gigantic taxation measure of the war. The National Bank Act, moreover, which has fortunately given us the best system of banking ever enjoyed by the country, was in reality recommended to Congress with the hope that it would facilitate the sale of United States bonds and aid our tottering credit. We blundered egregiously; but our vast resources made it possible to blunder without much suffering. Then, since all our national questions come before the voters, the country was obliged to listen to discussions in Congress, in the newspapers, and on the "stump," to very difficult problems of foreign trade, currency, and finance. Out of our very blunders, and from this revelation to the people of its ignorance, its inability to know how to meet the demands of a great emergency period, rose a desire, slowly growing throughout the community, as the recognition of the want was felt, to learn something of economics, and to study the principles which underlie the material prosperity of the nation. Out of the conscious-ness of weakness developed in the struggle came a natural longing for strength. The political leader who spoke, the journalist who discussed, the citizen who listened and read, all began to lament their want of training, and to admit the need of wholesome and sound instruction. The wish to speak intelligently on every subject which is uppermost in men's minds is a work-ing factor in the nature of all Americans; and the constant reference to economic questions in the journal which lay on the breakfast-table was at once a constant reminder to the reader of his ignorance and a laudable stimulus toward bet-ter knowledge of such subjects. The parent became anxious that the son should have the training which he had never got; and the new generation is now responding to this feeling.

In fact, it is now unquestionable that a new

interest in economics and finance has already arisen, and the cause of it seems to be very clear. The Civil War was, so to speak, the convulsion which brought into existence a desire for the study of political economy in the United States. The country was stirred to its depths by economic questions; for they entered into the political issues of exciting campaigns. The war issues thus did for the United States—in a different way, of course—even more than the corn-law agitation did for England. They actually gave birth to new motives for study. There never has been a time in our history when there was so evident a desire to get light on the economic problems of the day as now. There is a new stir among the ranks of the young men at college; and the printing-press sends forth an increasing flood of new books upon subjects which are constantly discussed in the daily newspapers. There is, without doubt, a new-born but slowly growing attention by the younger men of our land to the necessity—as well as the duty—of fitting themselves properly for the responsibilities of citizenship. In every social class, and in every department of business, men are eagerly asking for information on economic topics. If the war has given us this —the absence of which used to be so often lamented by thoughtful men a few years ago— then may some of our sacrifices not have been in vain. In that case the wind-shaking has surely resulted in abundant fruit.

To the minds of some persons the tangible evidences of this movement may not have been shown ; but it will not be difficult to give visible proof to such people. In the present awakening in educational discussion, one phase of which has been called the "Greek Question," it is worth while to notice the influence of the war period on the college curriculum. In most of our schools and colleges, on the breaking out of the war—and even to the present day—the pecuniary resources and endowments had been tied down by the provisions of donors, under the binding force of old traditions, to supply instruction in the customary Greek, Latin, mathematics, and philosophy, which were then considered the only essentials of a liberal education. But when, after tasting of the forbidden fruit of civil strife, our naked

3

ignorance was revealed to us, and when we looked about to see wherewithal our ignorance should be clothed, and in what schools the new studies could best be followed, it was discovered that the college curriculum (with a few exceptions) made practically no provision for such instruction. In the old days, when only sailing-vessels entered Boston harbor, but one channel, was practicable, and all the fortifications were placed in such a way as to command this single means of approach; yet, when steam took the place of sails, another channel proved the best, but it is now wholly undefended. The old ship-channel must be defended, but so must the new one. Likewise, in the case of collegiate studies, the old subjects are desirable, of course, but they are not the only desirable ones. The new demands, due to the progress of the age, must also be met. We shall, therefore, look with interest to see if the college curriculum shows any evidence of changes made to satisfy the new wants. As we look into the work of various institutions, these changes will be found to be very considerable. In fact, the response of the schools to the new demands is at once

the evidence and the result of the quickening
and stimulating conditions already described.
A comparison of the amount of instruction in
political economy given by the principal institutions of the land in 1860 and 1870 with that
given in 1884 will furnish us new proof that the
wind-shaken tree is yielding good fruit. (See
pages 28 and 29.)

When it is considered that the resources of
institutions have been generally hampered by
restrictions as to their use, this change in the
course of studies could have taken place only
by virtue of a very urgent pressure arising from
the public for such instruction. Nor can anything show more distinctly than the foregoing
tables how young is any real systematic study of
political economy in this country. It was not
likely that there could be any number of
trained economists among us in the days when
no serious attention was given to economic
study at the chief seats of learning. If it is
thought strange that we have had no "American school" of economists (except the followers
of Carey), there is a good reason for it in the
absence of any attempt to stimulate the best of

	1860.	1870.	1884.
Yale College..	One third of senior year.	One third of senior year.	1. *Elementary Course.*—Fawcett. Discussions on currency, banking, and taxation. Three hours a week for thirteen weeks. 2. *Elementary Course.*—Mill. Currency, banking, and taxation. Two hours a week for a year. 3. *Advanced Course.*—Discussion of economic problems and fallacies, with selections from leading treatises. Two hours a week for twenty weeks. 4. *Graduate Course.*—Finance and the art of politics, as illustrated in the history of the United States. Two hours a week for two years. 5. *Graduate Course* (in alternate years).—In 1883–1884, sociology. In 1884–1885, industrial history, history of political economy, finance, and theory of rights. One hour a week for each year. 6. History, business methods, and social problems of railroads. Two hours a week for a year. [A course about equal to courses 1 and 2 is given in the Sheffield Scientific School.]
Cornell University.	[Institution not founded.]	One third of junior year.	1. *Elementary Course.*—Lectures and recitations. Two hours a week, two thirds of a year. 2. Lectures on political economy. Five hours a week, one third of a year. 3. Lectures on finance.
University of Michigan.	Not in the course of study.	One term of senior year.	1. *Elementary Course.*—Lectures. Three hours a week, one half of a year. 2. *Advanced Course.*—Competition, free-trade and protection, commercial depressions, transportation, etc. Three hours a week, one half of a year. 3. Principles and methods of finance. Banking, national debts, etc. Two hours a week, one half of a year. 4. History of industrial society. Two hours a week, one half of a year. [Not given in 1883–1884.] 5. Financial seminary. History of American finance. Two hours a week, one half of a year. [Not given in 1883–1884.]

Columbia College.	Elective in one part of senior year.	One term of senior year.	1. *Elementary Course.*—Principles of political economy. Rogers's "Manual." Two hours a week, one half of a year. 2. History of politico-economic institutions. Two hours a week, one half of a year. 3. Finance and taxation. Two hours a week, one half of a year. 4. Statistical science, methods, and results. Two hours a week, one half of a year. 5. Communistic and socialistic theories. Two hours a week, one half of a year. [Topics like railways, banks, etc., are placed under administrative law.]
Harvard University.	One half of senior year.	1. Rogers's "Manual." One half of junior year, required. 2. Elective course for seniors: Adam Smith, Mill, Bowen. Three hours a week for a year.	1. *Elementary Course.*—Mill's "Political Economy." Lectures on banking and the financial legislation of the United States. Three hours a week for a year. 2. *Advanced Course.*—History of political economy. Cairnes, Carey, George, and recent literature. Three hours a week for a year. 3. Investigation of practical questions of the day. Banking, money, note issues, bimetallism, American shipping, etc. Three hours a week for a year. 4. Economic history since the Seven Years' War. Three hours a week for a year. 5. Land-tenures in England, Ireland, France, and Germany. One hour a week for a year. 6. History of tariff legislation in the United States. One hour a week for a year. 7. Comparison of the financial system of France, England, Germany, and the United States. One hour a week for a year. [Omitted 1884-1885.] 8. History of financial legislation in the United States. One hour a week for a year.

our youth to devote themselves to this branch of learning. But no excuse for a lack of train- ing can now be made, and there is hope that the present generation will give evidence of having made good use of its better opportuni- ties.

But apart from questions of training, there is a peculiar interest in the present position of political economy. It is one of the high- est attractions of a branch of study that the student can enter it as one of a body of scholars who are still acting as discoverers and investigators.   All of the results of political economy are not yet finally settled ; and al- though its outlines are fairly laid, within which any progress must be carried out, it offers the peculiar charm to an ambitious mind that some- thing may yet be done toward shaping its edifice into fairer proportions. Particularly does the new field in this wide country, of varying re- sources, offer tempting opportunities for special studies on our own economic conditions, and in the application of principles to the mass of in- dustrial facts around us.

The whole trend of civilization, moreover, is

in the direction where such studies will be more and more useful. In past centuries governments, in an unsettled state of society, found their chief concern lie in an attention to questions affecting life and property. Now that Christianity and the progress of enlightened ideas of government have made life and liberty more secure, in these later years legislation has concerned itself rather with property than life. A few centuries have made a great change in this respect. In the Middle Ages, while robber barons gained an income by an investment in castles, retainers, and arms, trade was regarded as plebeian: to fight, or to oppress, was considered as more noble than to encourage production, or work for the improvement of the poor. In the changed industrial conditions of to-day, castles have become factories; retainers, productive laborers; and arms, the hammers and tools of the artisan; while the affairs of peaceful trade and the increase of wealth are the chief causes of solicitude in the modern State. In the Southern States, for example, we have disposed forever of a question of human liberty in regard to the slaves—a bit of mediævalism—and in that part of our land we have turned our faces toward economic problems. How can the South best use its rich land, its timber, and its fine mineral resources? These are the new questions. By the alembic of war, and by the inevitable increase of population and wealth, our public measures have, in truth, become almost entirely economic.

To one who has not reflected on this matter, it is almost surprising to be told that national measures are now of a kind that require for their intelligent treatment some other training than that of a lawyer, to say nothing of the irrelevancy of service in the army. But mere lawyers and soldiers will no longer do for legislators. Consider the character of the questions at this time pressing upon Congress for consideration, and which are fraught with serious results to the business interests of the whole country. If we omit the administrative and political legislation on the Civil Service, the succession to the Presidency, and a National Bankruptcy Law, the remaining questions before Congress to-day are almost entirely economic.

1. There is, in the first place, the false sil-

ver dollar, masquerading in sheep's clothing, waiting to catch the unwary business world napping, when it will gradually assume its true depreciated character and devour from 15 to 18 per cent of all creditors' dues as estimated at present prices. The common laborers, moreover, receiving at first the same money wages as now, will find, when prices have risen to the depreciated silver standard, that they must bring about a new adjustment, entailing strikes, misunderstandings, and loss, until their wages shall rise to a sum sufficient to buy again as much as they do now. Laborers can not believe that their wages are so high as to be willing to suffer this losing game to go on. What has Congress done with this urgent question? Just what it did in the last months of 1861, and the early part of 1862, when it left the country to drift, unaided and undirected, upon the shoals of depreciated paper money. Monometallists and bimetallists, business men and bankers, have been all alike assaulting the dangerous silver legislation, but yet Congress has remained a very Gibraltar, in which the silver owners, supported by those who favor a cheap unit

with which to pay their debts, are securely in-
trenched.

2. Next, there is the banking question.　The
United States is a great commercial country, and
its business interests will grow with its population and wealth; and these interests are inex-
tricably wound up with banking and the ability
to obtain loans.　Nothing can be more delicate
and sensitive than the machinery of banking
and credit in any community; and yet men, to
satisfy the prejudices of their constituents, handle this mechanism with about the same air of
cheerful indifference as that which character-
izes a child when dragging around a rag doll by
the heels.　Persons of limited horizon live too
entirely in the present; they do not see that the
present has grown out of the past.　In the old
days of vicious and changing systems of banking, different in different States, no one knew
what bank-note was good, and our faith was
pinned on the statements in a "Bank-Note De-
tector," issued frequently enough to meet the
changing values of the State-Bank issues.　We
know little to-day of the losses suffered by note-
holders in those former times; for the present

National Bank system absolutely secures the note-holder against any loss, and because a note issued in Vermont is equally good in Oregon or Texas, these notes give a stability to trade in every part of the Union. And yet the whole problem of banking in the United States is unsolved. It is at present based upon a deposit of United States bonds, which are fast being paid off by our surplus revenues. What basis shall we adopt as a security for notes when the national debt is quite extinguished? This is a matter which vitally concerns every citizen who has any business stake in our land.

3. Again, Congress has been struggling with the most difficult of all problems—national taxation; the most difficult, because, even if the best policy were perfectly seen, there is an endless conflict of interests, placing us in great danger of passing under a rule of the strongest interests, not under the rule of impartial justice. We must resolutely face the fact that a re-examination of our whole scheme of taxation can not be any longer deferred. The heavy taxation burdens imposed during a time of war and peril, to the fullest extent that the country

could stand, were demanded by the presence of large armies in the field which were destroying wealth without creating it. The whole situation has changed. There have been twenty years of peace. The national debt has been reduced one half; and, instead of being obliged in 1867 to raise taxes to pay annually $143,000,000 of interest on the public debt, we are obliged in 1883 to collect only $59,000,000. The change to a peace footing means a readjustment of all branches of taxation; one can not be diminished by itself, any more than we should consent to remove the winter clothing from the right side of the body when summer comes and leave the left side still in winter array. The question, therefore, involves a decision upon the retention of internal taxes on distilled spirits and tobacco; of import duties on materials of manufacture and the articles of the laborer's consumption; of the management of our surplus revenue; and the whole sub-treasury system. It is a serious task, as imperatively demanded as it is difficult of execution. It calls for a knowledge of taxation methods in other countries than our own; and offers a tempting field for ener-

getic and manly endeavor. In the coming years
the tariff will be one of the chief political issues,
and as never before will it be discussed purely
on economic grounds. Hitherto the question
has been, Shall heavy customs-duties be levied
for revenue with which to continue the war, or
pay off the war-debt? Now the question is, since
the originating cause has disappeared, Shall the
tariff be retained because, purely in itself, it is
economically best for the whole interests of
the country?

4. But, perhaps, no matter excites more sen-
timental interest than the story of the rise of
our merchant shipping until about the year
1856, and of the subsequent steady and per-
sistent decline of our tonnage to the present
day. Out of conditions originating a century
ago enactments have found their way into our
statutes which are as much out of place as snow
storms in June. A junto of selfish interests
unite to protect these barbarisms. Ship-build-
ers are engaged in an industry the products of
which (ships) are absolutely forbidden importa-
tion into the United States, not even if duties
are paid on them as on the products of other

4

industries.   Such a prohibition exists for no
other article.   Moreover, owners of vessels, curiously enough, are exposed to open competition
in our own ports on equal terms with the citizens of other countries in all parts of the
world; but the foreigner is permitted to come
into our ports with a carrying instrument,
bought in whatever country he may buy it
most cheaply, while the American owner must
buy his ships here, where the cost per ton is
very much greater than abroad.   In this way,
with an instrument costing an American more
money than it does the foreigner, the foreigner
is nevertheless now permitted to compete with
him without restrictions.   No wonder ship-mas-
ters can not carry as cheaply as foreigners, even
if they exact no lower rate of profit; no wonder
the percentage of exports and imports carried
in American vessels has dwindled—apart from
the influences of other bad laws—from 82.9 per
cent. in 1840 to 15.5 per cent. in 1882.   The
problem of our shipping needs the touchstone
of some wider training than is furnished by self
ish individual interests.   Our self-complacency
may be soothed, perhaps, by the reflection that

the preservation of injurious laws on the statute-books is a marked characteristic of conserva-tism, even in a republic.

5. Discussions on the nature and value of paper money have formed an important part of political campaigns in the past, and it had been hoped that the paper-money demon had been laid. The inflation and contraction of our circulating medium were the shibboleths of hostile camps, who almost monopolized public attention for some years. It was once thought that our legal-tender notes were a temporary re-source, made possible at the most only in time of war and distress; but we can no longer feel that this position is a refuge. The Supreme Court, by the decision of Judge Gray, has most unfortunately decided that Congress has the power to issue legal-tender notes in times of peace and when under no stress of a war neces-sity; a situation all the worse, because Congress is made the sole judge of the necessity for the issue. As matters now stand, all the trouble-some and intricate discussions on the question of paper money, which we once thought had been settled forever, are still possibilities of

the future, and, if Congress should so choose, it might repeat at this day all the errors which have made the words "continental currency" a by-word for absence of value. It would be discouraging to think that the same battle must be fought over again, were it not that we recognize the lack of simple and elementary instruction on these subjects in the only schools where the mass of our voters are educated. At present, the newspaper and the political speaker are the only means of instruction on these subjects which reach the majority of the American people. The common schools give no teaching on such essential matters. And on the question of the best circulating medium for the United States there will be wanted, in the future, the best learning and the best ability of this and the coming generations. The present state of affairs can only be a temporary one; we do not have one thing or the other, a policy for or against our present Government issues. We simply acquiesce, because they give us no trouble for the time being.

6. A farmer with a large orchard scarcely notices the loss of a few apples; but when

poachers actually extend their operations to taking away his trees, the sources of his wealth, he is likely to become more vigilant. In much the same way, it may be said that the United States is becoming interested in the policy of our public-land system. We are lately awakening to the fact that we have had no consistent economic policy in regard to our public lands and the settlement of our vast Western domain; and yet, as concerns the principles of land tenures and of the distribution of wealth, a lack of policy is of momentous interest to our country. The public lands are rapidly drifting out of the hands of the general Government, and no one seems to have cared much what disposition was made of them. Now that they are nearly gone, now that the dwindling is apparent, we are coming to interest ourselves in their fate; but the possibilities of good are fast disappearing under the cloud of accomplished facts, where nothing can be done. Will an educated public opinion make land-thieving too bold a process to warrant an attempt at it? We laud the ownership of homes by workmen; we hear much talk of the nationalization of land in place of private property; but there is little attention given to the question whether the "unearned increment" might not be retained in the case of land which has never as yet become private property. Would it not be to the interest of social safety to encourage the existence of a large body of yeomen resident on the land? Here are matters needing grave and serious consideration.

7. The questions of the day of an economic character are startlingly large in their importance. The mere mention of the word "railway" brings before the mind a congeries of difficult questions affecting western farmers, the ability of the State to regulate freight and passenger charges, and in short the whole vexed discussion of State interference. Railways afford probably the largest field of investment in the country, and the settlement of a policy of supervision and regulation for them will affect the wealth and income of unnumbered small shareholders in every part of the Union. No other branch of industry affects so large a number of our population, directly or indirectly. And yet a supine public allows

Congress to rush bills of vital importance through the various steps to final enactment without debate or due consideration, and—so far as most people are concerned—in perfect ignorance of the motives which caused the legislation.

8. It will, doubtless, be wearisome to more than mention the topics of Postal Telegraph, Chinese Labor, Strikes, Trades Unions, Communism, Co-operation, and Commercial Crises, all of which demand present attention, because every day we are acting in regard to them on either a good or a bad conception, yet for whose treatment the nicest discrimination and knowledge are constantly demanded.

9. But, so far, I have confined myself to speaking of public economic questions concerned only with our domestic relations. Leaving these behind, however, we shall find quite as important problems pressing for solution in regard to our intercourse with other countries. So long as we were the only civilized people of any moment on the Western Continent, the position we were to take toward our neighbors never gave us much need for reflection. Mean-

while, the growth of modern commerce, the expansion of populous areas north and south of us, the discovery of great mineral wealth outside of our own limits, inviting our enterprise and capital, has forced upon us the consideration of reciprocity with Canada, Mexico, and the West Indies. We have refused reciprocity to Canada, but we are considering the desirability of granting closer commercial relations with Mexico, and are dallying with the Spanish West Indies. People are asking what is the reason for a reciprocity treaty? What part does it form in any consistent scheme of intercourse with foreign nations? And here, again, economic information is demanded by the community.

From this brief outline of the questions of the day, it is easily seen how imperative a demand exists for economic training, should any one aspire to become a member of our National Legislature, or even to cast an intelligent vote for such a member to represent us in it. These are matters which should necessarily be made subjects of instruction in our schools and colleges. That a majority of public measures are economic is, from the foregoing review, a proposition which no one can impeach. Consequently, a heavy responsibility lies upon our institutions of learning to meet the new demands in a fitting manner, and upon the youth of the land to get adequate preparation for their civic duties.

I could wish, however, that these were the only reasons why Americans should be obliged to secure economic training, or why our educational forces should be strengthened on this side. But stronger reasons exist, in my opinion, than any that have been mentioned. These are to be found in what I may call the *economic portents.* To the present time we have been usually known as a "young country," which to the economist implies an abundance of cheap or unoccupied fertile land, a relatively scanty population, large returns to capital, and generally high wages. A full knowledge of our resources has not practically been reached as yet. These splendid resources and the lusty health of our young country have made it possible, to the present time, for legislators to blunder with impunity. With great industrial productiveness, due to an embarrassment of natural riches

and the industrial capabilities of our people, labor
and capital, while constantly receiving larger returns, would not naturally be over-critical and
hostile to each other. These things were a social
protection from class antagonisms. But is it
not possible that we are soon to reach a stage
when the strength of this protection will be
gradually reduced? Consider what is happening yearly. The young-country theory of the
past has led to the encouragement of unlimited
immigration, because, it was said, our prairies
should be settled and our towns should be built
up. Streams of foreigners have been arriving
on our shores, until it is not unlikely that we
are already beginning to find the proportion of
population to land a less favorable one than
heretofore. These new-comers, moreover, do
not in fact all go upon the land, but remain in
the cities, like standing pools of dirty water in
the streets, instead of being drawn off entirely
to the country districts. Indeed, the importa-
tion of uneducated, un-American, unrepublican
workmen from foreign lands is a problem in
itself, and calls loudly for some political and
economic qualification before these aliens should

be admitted to the franchise. But, whether voters or not, these men reek with the doctrines with which they have been saturated in European socialistic resorts. Such of them as come here stay in the cities: they have no dreams of work on the freshly-turned soil where Heaven gives a plentiful harvest to honest labor. Lawless communism—it is said advisedly—feeds on bad workmen. A saving mechanic is never a communist. Whatever we have to fear from social ferments, wild antagonisms of class against class, riotous disturbances, secret drilling under arms, is to be charged against persons of the former description.

But this is by no means the true ground of distrust in the future. Whenever the time comes—and come it must—when the "young-country" situation is well behind us; when, by an increasing population and a closer settlement, our land is fully occupied; when our special resources show some diminution in their richness; when labor and capital both get smaller rewards—then, unless economically trained, even honest men, finding themselves cramped by barriers of their own creation, but brought into operation by natural laws, will not know what is really happening, and in entire ignorance of the truth may fly in the face of law and wreak signal damage on society as the supposed cause of their evil situation. They may then be led into doing in the United States some of the things they are now doing in Europe. The day when this may happen with us is more or less distant, but it is coming nearer in proportion as the methods of men accustomed to social conditions in old and crowded countries are brought here by a never-ending stream of immigration.

The necessary inference from this exposition must, it seems to me, be very clear to all. We must get ready to give economic instruction of a simple and elementary kind in every common school in the country, in such a way that it shall reach the ordinary voter, and influence the thinking of the humblest workman. The State Legislatures should move in the matter, and insert the study at first in the high schools, and later into the lower grades. The experiments of William Ellis in the Birbeck schools in England show that the suggestion is not at all visionary ; and it is the duty of intelligent men in the community to make this demand upon the schools. He who feels any stake in the experiment of free government on this continent would fail of his whole duty did he not urge this plan as the only proper means to enable each man fittingly to perform his duties as a citizen.

We have seen that the war has plunged us into the consideration of gigantic questions of an economic character, and that the growth of our country in numbers and wealth is making a true understanding of such matters more neces- sary than ever to the prosperity of the nation ; and we have noticed that, as a result of the national wind-shaking, a rising tide of new in- terest in such studies is becoming unmistaka- bly evident everywhere. But the disheartening fact is no less true that these new and impera- tive demands are met only by meager and in- adequate means in the chief seats of learning, to say nothing of smaller schools and colleges. It is a surprising fact that in some of the most im- portant institutions (even including those whose courses were given in this chapter) there is no settled instructor in this branch of teaching. It is a fact of my experience that the best men of

5

the university, who would naturally incline to it, can not now find a career in economic teaching, because so few positions exist in this country as honorable rewards for the industry and learning of ambitious students. Men find a profession in teaching Greek and Latin, but not in teaching political economy. Above all ought it to be possible to find groups of the ablest of our young men collected at the universities, engaged in advanced economic study, writing monographs and investigating home problems, quite as much as they should study the geology or mineralogy of our own land. We have not yet really shown what kind of stuff Americans are made of for economic work. Stimulate investigation and conscientious study on American problems, and then we shall probably hear less of the absence of any school of economists among us.

Of the character of the study of political economy, the mental qualities brought into play, and the methods of approaching the subject, the reader will find an explanation in the following chapters.

CHAPTER II.

THE CHARACTER OF POLITICAL ECONOMY AS A STUDY.

WALTER BAGEHOT once said of certain literary economists, who had no bent for practical affairs, that they were "like astronomers who had never seen the stars." In fact, no small number of people believe that this applies to all political economists; that they do very well as students of books, but are unable to keep their heads in the midst of facts and actual business; and that only the "hard-headed" merchant is competent to explain to the uninitiated the causes of what he sees. As in many general beliefs, there is something just and right in this; and yet there is something too which is not included in it, which leads the holder of the belief to narrow and illiberal conclusions in regard to a very important study. A fair and candid consideration should be given to the qualities of mind called into play by the study of political economy, and then we may more easily judge of the character of the work demanded of an economist, and of the way in which these demands have been met.

It is axiomatic that not every person can succeed in political economy any more than in art or music. Some people, although admirably equipped in other directions, have begun the study of political economy with great zeal, only to realize finally that anything beyond a certain general knowledge and use of its principles is denied to them. Any hint, therefore, although imperfect as mine may be, of a knowledge of the mental qualities requisite for success in such a study, will at least set to thinking those who propose to begin it, and possibly lead those who do not intend to study it to consider whether they have formed a right judgment upon the work already accomplished by economists.

The mental qualities brought into use by political economy are of two seemingly opposite kinds; and, simply because of this distinct opposition between them, it seldom happens that many persons combine them both to great per-

fection, and consequently few persons have
achieved great success in the study. To illustrate best the mental operations required, let me
first recount briefly the process followed in an
economic investigation. Certain phenomena are
observed, and their accuracy ascertained: an
hypothetical explanation deduced from existing
principles of political economy, or a statement
of the cause operating to produce the observed
phenomena, is made on the best possible ground
known to the investigator; a process of verification then follows, wherein the hypothetical
principle is applied to other observed economic
facts; and, if it explains the given conditions in
all known cases to which it is applied, the law
is considered established—just as we proceed to
discover a law in physics (although the economic law is not capable of quantitative accuracy
in statement like the physical law). First, there
is observation, then deduction * from the basis

* Deduction is the process of reasoning from a general to a
particular, and is opposed to *induction*, as thus defined by Mr.
Mill: "The process by which we conclude that what is true of
certain individuals of a class is true of the whole class, or that
what is true at certain times will be true in similar circumstances
at all times," "System of Logic," book iii, chap. ii, § 1. In the

of established laws, in order to explain the observed facts, and lastly inductive verification,
with a severe and exacting standard. Or, to
again use the words of Bagehot, we act as if a
man were arrested under suspicion of murder:
a murder was known to have been committed,
and the doer of the crime has been suspected;
and then, if, on resort to legal and just proof, the
suspicion is found correct, he is declared guilty.
Likewise, when economic phenomena are observed, the law expressing the relation between
cause and effect is suspected; and if, on com-

earliest stage of economic science induction was used, as in the
physical sciences, whose history is thus described : "A long
period of laborious inductive research, during which the ground
is prepared and the seed sown, terminating at length in the discovery—most frequently made at nearly the same time by several
independent inquirers—of some one or two great physical truths ;
and then a period of harvest, in which, by the application of deductive reasoning, the fruits of the great discovery in the form
of numerous intermediate principles, connecting the higher principles with the facts of experience, are rapidly gathered in. . . .
But it is not in the discovery of *axiomata media* only that the po-
tency of the deductive process has been exemplified. . . . Of
this the most eminent example is the law of gravitation itself,
arrived at by Newton in the main by way of deduction, from the
dynamical premises supplied by Galileo." The problem was "to
find a force which, in conjunction and in conformity with the laws
of motion, will produce the planetary movements, already general-
ized by Kepler." Cairnes, "Logical Method," pp. 84, 85.

parison with the facts, this law is wholly sub-
stantiated—as it were, " found guilty "—it is
considered established.

By the deductive part of the process, the
logical and reasoning powers are called forth in
a marked degree. Hence economic study
needs, and in its processes gives, the discipline
of the severer logical and mathematical subjects. And some years of observation in the
class-room warrant the statement that, as a
rule, he who enjoys and masters mathematical
and logical work will succeed with political
economy, provided he has to some extent also
the other necessary mental qualities. What
these other qualities are may be seen by considering that, in the verifying part of the process
above described, an imperative need exists for
an honest, practical *appreciation of facts*, such as
is possessed by merchants and men of affairs,
coupled with an *economic intuition*, a faculty
which is more or less inborn. Whether this
economic intuition is a matter of cultivation or
not, I do not feel that my experience is extended
enough to decide; but I am inclined to the belief that it is. The capacity to collect and ar-

range facts is a book-keeper's function; but the
ability to see through the confusing mass of details and trace the operation of a governing
principle requires an intuitive regard for facts
and their causes possessed in a large measure
hitherto by only a few men.

If this analysis be a true one, it will appear
distinctly how it is that qualities almost diamet-
rically opposed to each other are necessary for
the equipment of an economist of the first rank.
On the one hand, he must have the power of
close, sustained, and logical reasoning; on the
other, he must have a most thoroughly practical
spirit, without vagaries and nonsense. The former he gains chiefly by his academic training;
the latter, by general maturity and an intuitive
or practical knowledge of the world of business.
In short, he must be at once a (so-called) "doctrinaire" and a "practical man." To be without one set of these faculties is to seriously and
fatally prevent any great usefulness. A purely
"practical man," without the logical training,
can no more achieve economic success than a
railway-locomotive, no matter how great its
steam-power, can continue to run and reach its

destination without rails. And yet, a bookish and literary economist, without the practical intuitions, can accomplish nothing more than a finely finished and most perfect engine in the hands of an ignoramus who does not know how to get up steam.

We here find the explanation of a very common belief among the wide ranks of the busy and successful men of affairs in the United States—a class who have generally had little academic training — that economists are mere " doctrinaires," whose assumptions are all *a priori*, all in the air, and above the level of every-day work; who had better make a fortune in pig-iron, or fancy dress-goods, before they set up to instruct the community. Merely making money, however, does not at the same time make one logical. It is as if we should demand that every scientific physicist or chemist should have first put his knowledge into practice by inventing an automatic brake, or a patent-medicine, before he is competent to impart the principles of his science to others. The contempt of the practical world for (so-called) " doctrinaires" is as great a mistake as for the

speculative writers to set themselves above the
men of affairs. As in most questions involving
both mental and material considerations, the
just position lies somewhere between these
extreme views. If an economist is an abstract thinker, and nothing else — unable to
verify his deductions — then he justly merits
contempt; but in that case he is not a properly equipped man, as we have described him
above. On the other hand, it is common
to see merchants or manufacturers showing
great energy in studying and writing upon economic subjects, who, so long as they confine
themselves to the range of facts within the
limits of their own horizon, make most valuable
and effective contributions to the verification of
principles; but, when, without accuracy, logical
power, or a grasp upon governing principles,
they begin to lay down general propositions
based on their limited knowledge of particular
facts, they are very apt to be less effective and
useful than they are dogmatic. They will find
that their general principle, owing to its insuf-
ficient basis, will conflict with truths already
established, and whose correctness they must

necessarily deny in order to make room for their little theory. He only is truly an economist who, eagerly studious of facts, not in one occupation or place only, but in as many as possible, applies scientific processes to his investigation, and produces that which becomes the world's truth, the property of men of all times —not the petty sum of thought which comprehends only a small fraction of the facts. In other words, when a wide-awake man goes to books, he really goes to get the experience of the best observers of all countries with which to correct himself against false and narrow inferences drawn from his own limited experience.

In order to show how far this analysis is based on experience, I shall appeal to the history of the work of the most successful economists. Such an historical survey will, in my opinion, give results of an interesting and instructive kind. Adam Smith, Ricardo, Mill, and Cairnes combined in a high degree the two almost opposite kinds of powers needed for their success; and these men have made the most considerable contributions to our present knowledge of economic principles.

It would be hard to name an author who has wielded a greater influence by his writings than Adam Smith by his " Wealth of Nations " (1776). His work was a great and admitted success, as tried by any tests, whether of popularity or permanent influence on men's minds. But on his tombstone will be found inscribed the name of an extensive ethical work, " The Theory of Moral Sentiments," as an equal claim to distinction with the " Wealth of Nations." What is worth noting about this is that the great writer was a Professor of Moral Philosophy in Glasgow, and had planned an extensive course of lectures in which political economy formed but one part ; and we find that by training, by aptitude, by study, he was a skillful master of logic ; he had the power to proceed from a given premise to its logical conclusion, and to see the principles which followed from the acceptance of a given position ; he could hold to an abstraction, in the form of general truth, unweighted by the concrete accidents of form in which it might be at any time working ; and it was his pre-eminent ability in securing a firm grasp upon principles, apart from their applica-

tion, which gave him later a scientific and systematic control over his subject, and enabled
him to weld it into a compact and cohering
whole. It was this power which made it possible for him to lay the foundations of a science
of political economy. It widened his views,
and made it easy for him to see the connection
of one part of truth with the whole. In short,
he possessed in a remarkable degree a logical
and philosophic faculty, the first of the two
requisites for successful economic work. But,
then, to an almost equal extent, he honestly
reverenced industrial and commercial facts; he
studied them eagerly, and made his book an extensive collection of data on many special subjects. Everywhere on his pages one meets with
the analysis and study of particular industrial
phenomena to which his principles were applied; and in them the keen, observing Scotchman, with a subtle, economic instinct, saw the
operation of laws where the ordinary man of
affairs saw only a crowd of familiar and mo-
notonous details of business. The practical nature of his work is so well known that it seems
unnecessary to call further attention to this side

6

of his make-up. So well has this been understood, that the late Cliffe-Leslie claimed for
Adam Smith that his method of working was
solely inductive, that is, by a method of reasoning directly from particular facts to the general
truth. A more liberal view of all the powers
and surroundings of the great economist will
not allow us to agree to this. And, as we try
to take in the whole man, rather than any part
of him, we are brought to the broader conclusion that it was, without question, the union of
a philosophic and logical faculty, which enabled
him to deduce his principles from ascertained
premises, with a true and correct instinct in the
application of these laws to facts, which lay at
the bottom of Adam Smith's world-wide success
in his "Wealth of Nations." He had the power
to see the law working in the concrete; to disclose the operating force; to shake off the in-
cidental circumstances of its concrete envelope,
and, after verifying his conclusions, formulate
them in simple terms for use by others in subsequent explanations. The great Scotchman
was at once the prince of "doctrinaires," and
the most practical man of his time.

Curiously enough, while Adam Smith approached political economy from the side of abstract and metaphysical studies, his " homely sagacity " led him constantly to practical results, Ricardo approached the study as a rich banker and a successful man of business, who had early retired with a competence; but yet it was Ricardo who, above all others, went farthest in attempting to formulate the principles he had arrived at in a form which stated abstractly the general truths, independent of the changing conditions in which these principles worked. So that in him we have a man of economic intuitions of the most practical kind, but one who early showed a fondness for mathematics and logical studies. Knowing only too well the myriad shapes in which facts arise before us, he was urged forward by a desire to express truth in a form as succinct and universal as possible. This tendency of his mind, taken in connection with unusual terseness and no great literary skill in exposition, has deceived people, chiefly because of his dry and peculiar method of stating himself, into thinking that his conclusions were all based on unsubstantial premises; while,

as a matter of fact, he was a hard-headed man
of affairs, living at a time when the Bank of
England restriction act and the duties on corn
led him to try to find out the fundamental
principles which were governing the value of
money and the price of corn. The results of
these practical investigations were seen in the
doctrines of the " Bullion Report," and the economic doctrines of " Rent " and " International
Trade." *   In this way the work of the Scotch

---

* No one has been more attacked, and less understood, than
Ricardo. That he made proper use of the scientific methods can be
seen by a brief quotation.   In the following words Mr. Cairnes has
shown how he made use of hypothesis, which is analogous to experiment in the physical sciences : " The question under consideration
was the fundamental principle of international trade, and Ricardo
wished to show that it might be the interest of a country to import
an article from another, even though it were in its power to produce
the imported article itself at less cost than it was produced at in
the country from which it came.   This, at first view, paradoxical
position, Ricardo thus by means of a simple hypothesis (which,
while it divested the problem of all its accidental complications,
brought into clear light the few essential conditions on which its
solution depended) was enabled to establish ; it being evident
that, under the supposed circumstances, the known motives of
men in the pursuit of wealth could only lead to the very result
asserted.   ' Two men,' he says, ' can both make shoes and hats,
and one is superior to the other in both employments ; but in
making hats he can only exceed his competitor by one fifth, or 20
per cent., while in making shoes he can excel him by one third, or
33 per cent. ; will it not be to the interest of both that the supe-

Professor of Logic, who had a great deal of practical insight, was supplemented by the study of a successful man of affairs who had a strong passion for concise and abstract statement of economic principles. We can not properly say of the man who was introduced to the details of the money market at fourteen, was in business on his own account at twenty-one, and was a wealthy man at twenty-five, that he was a doctrinaire wholly given over to abstract speculations.

John Stuart Mill illustrates what we have said in a different way. To him the fascination of abstract reasoning was so great, and the bent of his mind so strongly metaphysical, that this part of the economist's equipment preponderated in his make-up; while his attention to the facts of practical life was not extensive. And this exposes whatever of weakness there is in his book. Perhaps no other systematic writer ever gained such success by perspicuous treatment, and a certain geometrical symmetry in the connection

rior man should employ himself exclusively in making shoes, and the inferior man in making hats?'" "Logical Method," pp. 93, 94.

of parts with a whole, as did Mr. Mill in his
" Principles of Political Economy," and this
quality has greatly added to the value of his
work.   But, while the abstract character of
many of his chapters excites admiration because
of the power of sustained reasoning which they
show, yet it must be confessed that they are
too often ill-adapted to the common apprehension.   Had he possessed more knowledge and
acquaintance with practical business life, been
nearer to the monotony of details, his work
might have been imbued with a smack of
practicality which would have redeemed its
abstractness, and made it vastly more useful.
Moreover, he would, as in the discussion of the
wages question, have adapted his principles
more correctly to the truth, and gained positions less likely to be assailed after others had
noted their too great symmetry and too few
limitations.   His early training accounts for his
book as it stands, and explains his faults.   Too
much stress should not, however, be laid on
what was only a partial lack in Mill's practical
experience.   Account must be taken of the life
Mill led as a servant in the East India Compa-

ny's office, which widened his horizon, gave his
mind practical employment, and furnished him
with a great field of experience in men and
things. This, without doubt, exercised a strong
and steadying influence on his thinking, which
had some of the faults of English insularity,
and, taken together with his robust philanthropy, gave that practical direction to his work
which, while it was inadequate, yet redeemed
him from the charge of being unduly given over
to abstractions. Had he had an interest in
work-a-day things which equaled his fondness
for metaphysics and abstract thinking, he would
have succeeded even more than he did, and he
made a great success. His treatment of international values is a conspicuous example of his
faculty for extended reasoning, but, had he put
it more as a practical man of affairs and less
in the form in which he originally worked it out,
he could have made a much better exposition
of the principles, and gained vastly in his hold
upon the reader. Does it not become evident,
then, that mere philosophic acumen is not sufficient in the model economist? But, on the
other hand, is it not evident that the ability of

a mere man of affairs is not sufficient to grasp the workings of principles in the confusion of details? These two sets of faculties must be, and always are, combined in him who accomplishes the best economic work.

The personality of Mill's great successor, Mr. Cairnes, is a very interesting one. He both knew and thought much. Members of Parliament would come to sit by his invalid's chair, in which he was confined by a painful disorder, finally ending in an untimely death, and find him more learned than they in the details and facts of certain legislation; yet with this accumulation of practical knowledge, for which he had a peculiar aptitude, no one since Ricardo has shown so vigorous a faculty for investigation, and the power of keeping his head while in the pursuit of principles. He was not befogged by metaphysical niceties, but saw his way through the complexity of actual business life with as sure and certain an insight into the actuating causes, and with as clear and definite a view of the principles in operation, as an expert accountant when adding a column of figures. In his little volume, " The Logical Method," in which he explains his ideas as to the processes to be followed in an economic investigation, his logical and philosophic side is most admirably seen. Nowhere else does he seem more clearly to show how essentially he had the power to handle a purely abstract question, such as that of method. And yet, on the other hand, it is to be noticed in his " Leading Principles " that the whole criticism, by which he amends Mr. Mill's positions—his study of value, the wages question, and international trade— shows how much more appreciation he had of the real facts of trade than Mr. Mill. Under the light of his economic insight the cold columns of Australian statistics and American exports and imports glow with brilliant illustrations of general economic laws. With a firm grasp upon principles, and the ability to see their operation in practical affairs, he examined the facts of our foreign trade before 1873, and came to the conclusion that we were rapidly accumulating the material for a great financial explosion—nay, he even actually prophesied the panic which came in that year. Scarcely any other economist affords a better illustration of the success

arising from the possession of these two almost
wholly unlike powers of mind which I have
been trying to show are essential for the high-
est achievement in political economy. Mr.
Cairnes was an economic tight-rope walker; he
could go with a cool head through airy spaces
where other men became dizzy or fell to the
ground. And, at the same time, he had the
Englishman's sturdy respect for facts, with
more than the ordinary Englishman's willingness to acquaint himself with social systems different from his own.

These economists, whose powers I have at-
tempted to analyze, have been the ones who
have contributed most to our knowledge of
the principles of political economy, as they
are understood to-day. Above all other writers,
these men have possessed a useful economic
intuition, and a respect for facts, which have
given peculiar strength to their clear, abstract
generalization of results in the form of universal principles. They have been able to reason from ascertained premises to conclusions
with steadiness and accuracy; and yet they
have been able to seek the facts for verification

and illustration. Wherever other students and writers have accomplished less, it will appear that weakness arose from their entire or partial lack of one or both of these two sets of faculties.

If my analysis is correct, it will explain some other things also. French writers are unexcelled in the power of lucid statement; but the generalizing and less practical French (although there are exceptions) are not so likely to be good economists as the more common-sense English. Therefore, although the French have stated results in the most admirable way, they have not originated so much as have the English. It is, then, reasonable also to expect that the practical Americans, with the keen insight of their men of affairs, may also furnish the material for excellent economists, whenever they set themselves seriously to get the proper systematic training. For, together with the zest for commerce, the Americans probably possess considerable aptitude for logical processes, if they care to cultivate themselves.

If my exposition is accepted, it will now be evident what sets of mental qualities are

most demanded by this study. It is desirable,
then, not only that he who thinks of beginning
political economy, but he who has already
given it some attention, should question whether he possesses the requisite ability for gaining
success. This, however, should not deter the
man of but average capacity from seeking an
elementary and general knowledge of its principles. His duty as a citizen demands that;
but he may well consider whether the preliminary work calls out in him any real interest,
and if he thinks of a future and extended course
of study, whether he can bring to it the qualities of mind above described.

CHAPTER III.

THE DISCIPLINARY POWER OF POLITICAL ECONOMY.

IT may now be worth while to explain briefly some of the evident ways by which the study of political economy disciplines the mind. To most persons economic knowledge is favorably recommended because of its extreme usefulness to every citizen who casts a ballot; but it will be found, I think, that its value as a mental exercise—apart from the desire to get useful information—is one of the main considerations to be kept in mind by students.

It may seem somewhat startling to say of so practical a subject that, in a pre-eminent degree, it calls for the exercise of imagination. "That is just what we have always said," the scoffers at political economy say at once; "so does novel-writing call for imagination, and a novel-

7

ist is about as well fitted for the economist's position as the usual abstract thinker who masquerades as a teacher of political economy." To this it is to be replied that imagination is one of the chief requisites for mathematical study also; that a novelist is not necessarily a good mathematician goes without saying. The simplest propositions of solid geometry require the exercise of imagination, as, for example, in the picturing of forms and solids with intersecting planes, while the most logical student of the severest mathematical processes is called on for the exercise of this species of imagination. Still, as Tyndall says, "There are Tories even in science who regard imagination as a faculty to be feared and avoided rather than employed. They had observed its action in weak vessels, and were unduly impressed by its disasters. But they might with equal justice point to exploded boilers as an argument against the use of steam. Bounded and conditioned by co-operant reason, imagination becomes the mightiest instrument of the physical discoverer. Newton's passage from a falling apple to a falling moon was, at the outset, a leap of the imagination." *

The use of the imagination is, in my opinion, still more necessary in political economy than in the natural sciences, or in mathematics. I have already alluded in another chapter to the place occupied in economic processes by hypothesis. The following case given by Mr. Cairnes † will furnish a good illustration: "If, for example, [the] purpose be to ascertain the relation subsisting between the quantity of money in circulation in any given area of exchange transactions and its value, [one] might make some such supposition as this: 1, in a given state of productive industry a certain

* "Scientific Use of the Imagination," in "Fragments of Science," p. 130. Tyndall himself, in the same essay (p. 149), makes use of the same intellectual "cart-horse" in speaking of the extreme tenuity of interstellar matter: "Suppose a shell to surround the earth at a height above the surface which could place it beyond the grosser matter that hangs in the lower regions of the air—say at the height of the Matterhorn or Mont Blanc. Outside this shell we have the deep-blue firmament. Let the atmospheric space beyond the shell be swept clean, and let the sky-matter be properly gathered up. What is its probable amount? I have sometimes thought that a lady's portmanteau would contain it all. I have thought that even a gentleman's portmanteau—possibly his snuff-box—might take it in."

† "Logical Method," pp. 90-91.

number and amount of exchange transactions to be preferred; 2, a certain amount of money in circulation; 3, a certain degree of efficiency (in the sense explained by Mr. Mill) in the discharge of its functions by this money; 4, lastly, a certain addition made to the money already in circulation. These conditions being supposed, and being also supposed to remain constant, the scene of the experiment would be prepared. It is true the action of the added money can not be made apparent to the senses of the economist, or to those of his hearers or readers, but from his knowledge of the purposes for which money is used, and of the motives of human beings in the production and exchange of wealth, it will be in his power to trace the consequences which in the assumed circumstances would ensue. These he would find to be an advance in the prices of commodities in proportion to the augmentation of the monetary circulation; a result from which he would be justified in formulating the doctrine that, other things being the same, the value of money is inversely as its quantity." From this it can be seen how prominent a part the exercise of the imaginations plays in an economic investigation. The physicist and the geologist make use of the same power, it is true, but it seems to be more important to the economist than to them. Very often, in order to show the action of a single principle operating by itself, we must separate all conflicting agencies from the situation—just as the physicist experiments in a vacuum exhausted of air, for the purpose of learning the full effect of a force, like gravity, when acting by itself. The economist, however, is not able to reproduce a given situation to the eye or ear, as is the physicist. He can not pile before him the exports of the United States or England, or summon before him the laboring-class or the capitalists of a country; he must, therefore, picture to himself the actual facts, just as the geometrician does the forms of a solid, and see how the operating principle works. This is very far from "theoretical dreaming." It is at once a most difficult process, and a most serious discipline in learning how to think on such subjects.*

* Expressing himself from a different point of view, Cliffe Leslie said: "Want of imagination is one of the causes of the inabil-

. Not only in the advanced methods of investigation, however, but in the most elementary economic study will the imagination be called into requisition. In beginning political economy, the perception of a simple general principle is often absurdly easy, but, for its assimilation into our own thinking, it is necessary that it should have become an interpreter of facts everywhere about us. To this end, it is essential for us to apply the abstaction, or general principle, in every possible case, to some concrete phenomenon. To illustrate my meaning in a simple way, it is one thing to say that in order to have value a commodity must satisfy some desire, and be hard to get; and quite another thing to be able to call up in the mind an image which will show the application of the principle. For example, to a shipwrecked sailor on a rocky island a bag of gold has no value, it can satisfy no desire, for it can not keep him alive. The student is absolutely forced to imagine to

ity of many economists to emancipate themselves from old abstractions, generalizations, and formulas. Their minds do not enable them to realize actual phenomena, and to test theories on all sides by a multitude of instances." "Political Economy in the United States," in "Fortnightly Review," October 1880.

himself concrete conditions whenever he is reading a statement of principles by an author; if he does not turn the subject into a reality in this way it will slip away from him like anything else on which he exercises merely his memory. If he is talking about rent, he must, by his imagination, keep before him a picture of a farm as it is in reality; he must call up the concrete in an image, and follow out the explanation of the writer, or lecturer, by seeing the changes which take place as the exposition proceeds. I can not too much emphasize the importance of this method to clear thinking and satisfactory progress in political economy. The student must be constantly at work with his imagination, making a series of illustrations of what he is reading.

It is largely by such mental exercise as this that a student best succeeds in assimilating the body of principles which make up the science of political economy. It has been frequently said to me, " I can understand the statements of the writer easily, but I do not seem to be able to use the idea when called upon to explain things in a different connection." This is exactly the difficulty, as it is also, by struggling with the difficulty, one of the best disciplinary gains of our study. If the student had conceived in his own mind an image of the principle working in some definite facts, he would not have complained in this way; the less so if he had tried it on more than one set of facts, and had seen how the principle operated in more than one supposed case. To understand an abstract principle, without the ability to see it in the concrete form, and test its truth, is of little gain to any one. This would in truth make a "doctrinaire." And we may now see somewhat more clearly the true value to be set on the claims of the much vaunted man who scorns everything but facts, historical facts. We ought now to be able to recognize that the only "practical man," in any conceivable sense known to economic science, is he who, while seeing general principles, can best interpret the facts around him. The position thus gained, consequently, gives us added means of seeing how economic study can be most intelligently carried on. To follow through a course of political economy without the attempt above described, to think out the principles by use of the imagination, and by constant application to familiar facts, would be like trying to climb a perpendicular wall of ice—the student will not catch hold.

Moreover, this kind of mental exercise is continually calling upon one for the ability to see the pivotal part in any statement, whether of fact or principle. Not to see the essential bearing of an exposition is a species of mental blindness; but exercise will gradually give clearer vision. Nothing is more common in the replies of untrained students to questions than the happy-go-lucky kind of answers which bear upon the general subject, but are aside from the point. Persons may write or speak *about* the question, but do not answer it; what they say may be quite true in itself, but it is irrelevant. The faculty of hitting a point, or *relevancy*, is one, in my opinion, like concentration of mind (to which it is nearly allied), which is largely capable of cultivation and growth. And the discipline of rigorous study in political economy is one of the best means of acquiring it. In my experience, there have been, I conceive, some interesting illustrations of this idea.

·Trained lawyers have, by heredity, transferred this faculty of directness of thought to their sons; and it has been possible, sometimes, without further data, to pick out the sons of lawyers from reading their examination-books in political economy. These young men "hit the nail on the head," and make clean work of their answers, without any mental shuffling, or avoidance of the essential point.

To make progress in such a study as political economy, the student must necessarily gain exactitude and clearness, both in writing and speaking. Nothing is more striking in the experience of an instructor, as he faces a new class, than the limited powers of expression possessed even by young men who have had, in most cases, a very extended course of classical training. It is largely due, of course, to vague and loose thinking. He who has clear ideas can generally manage to convey his meaning in varying degrees of force, correctness, and elegance. The necessity, however, of making clear distinctions between things, which at first seem all alike, to see forces operating where none were seen before, stimulates unused faculties, and then, as a natural result, progress becomes distinctly visible. Men who at the beginning expressed themselves in halting, inexact, and timid words, with a seeming passion for brevity, will, at the end of the course in which they have been constantly pushed to express themselves, talk easily and freely on subjects which would at first have frightened them by an appearance of abstractness. In this respect, the training must be much like that in the study of metaphysics. Under constant criticism looseness of words and definitions will disappear— as clearness of ideas comes in. In no other study is inexactitude or lack of precision in words or facts more likely to stir up criticism and ridicule than in political economy, because in no other study are we more concerned with things which affect all the world in every day of its existence, and in which absurd results and stupid mistakes are more easily seen by everybody. The economist must be vigilant and correct; and the results of this requirement are such as tend to keep him as careful and exact as is possible. The effect of training under such conditions can not fail to be admirable.

Again, the logical powers are constantly exercised and stimulated. Political economy will not, of course, make a man logical; but a student will feel the need of logical training and accuracy at every step. It will often happen that the intuition of the student will lead him to give a correct reply to a question regarding two things which have an apparent connection; but, if he should be called upon to give the logical chain of connection in every step, he will find the study a very different thing than he supposed. He will be taught to think. If he has been rigorously kept up to this process he will gradually get a faculty of reasoning with some ease about economic questions, and new problems will be better handled because of his experience in treating old ones. Every student will be able to mark his own progress, if he has honestly done this work as he went along, when he looks back over the course, and sees that earlier difficulties, which at the time seemed serious, have now little power to delay him.

As the logical part of the study naturally brings its discipline, so we may expect that its practical side will stimulate the student in such a way as will teach him greater regard for facts, and for the immediate interests of life. His economic intuition will grow, also, as he becomes familiar with the definitions and fundamental conceptions of the study. New practice will constantly develop new power, and new confidence. It goes without saying that this can not come at once, and that the man who is unwilling to exert himself can not get it. But, although severe logical processes are demanded, as in mathematics, yet the student will be attracted by the peculiarly human and practical element in the questions discussed, and he will be drawn on to exert himself by his interest in these matters. He will be willing to do more in a subject whose ends are intensely practical than in one removed from any application to his own personal conditions.

One other marked result of the study of political economy deserves at least passing mention. Persons who by nature are unfitted for other kinds of academic work, and yet by cus-

8

tom or authority have trodden the beaten educational paths with a dull sense of discouragement and incapacity, have, in many cases, been awakened to a hitherto unknown interest in study by the practical and interesting nature of the subject. Economic questions confront them everywhere, and they meet with their discussion over the table, on the walk, and in the newspapers. It, consequently, stimulates even a sluggish disposition to find that he can know something valuable about such practical matters of every-day importance. Livy or Thucydides may pall on his incapacity, but his curiosity may be piqued by having the functions of money explained to him. The purchasing power of his yearly allowance is something which comes home even to him. As enlarging the field for willing mental activity, and giving new and interesting objects for intellectual effort, political economy forms one of the most effective factors in the movement which in these latter days is liberalizing our courses of study, and is freeing us slowly from the cramped tyranny of a traditional training, still demanded, forsooth, because it once seemed good to the schoolmen. Willing, enthusiastic study, since it interests and fits the faculties, is a better thing for discipline than the serfdom of drudgery in a subject which excites no spontaneous response and stirs an unwilling effort. And this is true, also, without any thought of undervaluing other branches of study. We must all admit that some minds are better fitted for one thing than for another, and that we can not do all things equally well. There is, therefore, a place for different studies so long as human abilities remain of a varied kind, and room should not be denied to any branch of learning which, apart from its " usefulness," is effective for mental discipline.

A warning, however, should be given at the outset which may save later disappointment to some persons. No one would think of becoming an accomplished chemist or geologist in one course pursued for one year ; but many persons conceive that they can easily know all of political economy that is necessary for a sound judgment on current questions in a less time than that. It is true that they can read over the statement of principles in a less time, but they can not become economists so easily. To have been trained until these principles become as familiar as the alphabet requires time—time not merely for the intellectual efforts of applying the principles, but time for the mind to mature under the exertion and to digest its food slowly; since only by growth and experience can there come any development of the economic intuition and a power to call readily upon any part of one's acquisitions for instant use at any moment. This warning is not to be understood as deterring any one from an attempt to master the elements of political economy. A person of ordinary parts can by industry obtain an amount of knowledge which will not only be valuable to him as a citizen, and save him from errors, but it will give him discipline in the proportion of his application and energy. An elementary course will serve a distinct purpose as part of a liberal education for every citizen, but he will not become an economist "*teres atque rotundus*" at once. A brief course in chemistry may not enable the student to contribute immediately to a new theory of heat, but it may give him a highly useful knowledge of the chem-

istry of every-day things. We must not, therefore, expect more from a short study of political economy than we do from the same exertion in other serious studies.

CHAPTER IV.

THE RELATIONS OF POLITICAL ECONOMY TO THE LAW, THE MINISTRY, AND JOURNALISM.

POLITICAL economy holds a very close connection with THE LAW on different grounds.

In the first place, the disciplinary power of the study is very much that which is gained in the study and pursuit of the law. As has been already explained, the student of economies is chiefly concerned in getting a firmly-rooted understanding of principles, which he is then constantly engaged in applying to the phenomena around him. Or, struck by some new or interesting fact, he sets himself to find the causes of the effects he has observed. In thus applying general principles to explain special facts, the student of political economy is doing almost exactly that which the student of law does, when he applies legal principles to particular cases, or when he is considering

whether the interpretation of the law in a decision of the courts applies also to the special
case he has in hand.   The modern theory of
legal teaching no longer recognizes the wisdom
of simply filling the mind with statements of
what the law now is, but aims to force the
student, under oversight, to discover the principle running through multitudes of cases already decided, or constantly to apply principles
to given facts.   If this be a correct statement
of methods of teaching in the law, it will be
seen at once that the student goes through very
much the same mental operations as in the
study of political economy.   There is in fact
a striking similarity between the position of
the practicing lawyer and the economist; the
lawyer is faced with a statement of facts by his
client, to which, after he has sifted their accuracy, he tries to discover what legal principles
apply; or the court, after ascertaining the truth
of the averments on either side, then considers
the applicability of certain general principles of
law to them.   The economist in like manner is
brought to notice, for example, some practical
phenomena of banking, or prices; then he tests

the accuracy of the facts; and finally sets himself to discover what economic principles
explain the observed statistics. The mental
attitude of the student is thus almost exactly
the same in the two cases. There could, therefore—looking at the matter entirely from the
disciplinary point of view — scarcely be any
kind of study which would better train a man
for the mental processes of a lawyer's work
than political economy.

For another reason lawyers have a necessary interest in our study. Those who follow
the law are, in this country, most likely to be
chosen to make the law in legislative assem-
blies. Upon them will hang heavy responsibilities, apart from questions of law and administration; for they must represent the economic
interests of the country as well. From their
numbers, also, are generally recruited the active
campaign speakers in our election contests; and
it is becoming in them to study with care that
which they expect to declare to the people in
rhetorical sentences from the platform. Political science, which includes legal and constitutional history, international law, ethics, the

study of government, and political economy, is
a field of large importance in a land of popular
government, and the legislator ought to be
conversant, more or less intimately, with all its
branches—and especially with political economy. This reason for the study of economics
by the legal profession is the material one of
"usefulness," in the same way that a knowledge
of guns is necessary for an artillery officer.

Legal principles, moreover, are often based
on economic grounds, and their force is to be
gauged by their economic importance. Laws
of bargain and sale are of this class; so, too,
such as concern bills of exchange, and mercan-
tile operations. Parts of the law like these
stand in marked contrast to what is purely
legal and formal, as, for example, the affixing
of a stamp to a deed or mortgage. For the
interpretation and discussion of the former
principles, it is difficult to see how clearness
can be obtained without an adequate understanding of the underlying principles of political economy. This is a different thing, be it
noted, from the need of physics or chemistry
by the lawyer, in cases which hinge on a

knowledge of these subjects. A case, the facts of which require a more or less profound study of physics or chemistry to understand them, is settled by the application of legal principles, covering not this one case, but any case of a similar kind; and it is the insight into these principles affecting cases in general, and not the facts of any one special case, of which I am speaking.

The relation of political economy to THE MINISTRY is of an entirely different nature. To the ministry are relegated, rightly or wrongly, in a great degree, questions of ethics. It is true that students of ethics exist outside of the ministry, but theirs is the one profession which is expected to see that some kind of ethics is put into practice by the individual.

At the outset, we must learn that practical ethics begins where political economy leaves off. It is not desirable here to discuss whether or not such a branch of science exists as sociology; but there is certainly a growing feeling in favor of confining economics strictly to questions of wealth, as a means of reaching as exact conclusions as possible by a limitation of the field of inquiry. This is the only legitimate sphere of our study. When the economist has made clear that given social regulations have certain material effects for good or for evil on the welfare of any class in the community, then it is in order for others to take up the matter where political economy left it, and set themselves to discover the practical means by which mind and character may be acted upon, so as to bring about the good and avoid the evil results which political economy has shown must follow from stated conditions. This practical ethical work does not fall within the proper province of the economist; but if—owing to the fact that economic studies are as yet in their infancy, and that branches of thought closely dependent on political economy are supposed only to be known by economists—popular opinion forces the economist also to perform the function of a teacher of ethics, or of a social philosopher, it should be kept distinctly in mind that in this case he has stepped over the boundaries of his own science, and is for the time being within the limits of another—although an allied—study.

It is true, of course, that the same man might be fitted to be both an economist and an ethical teacher; and this was the *rôle* adopted by both Adam Smith and John Stuart Mill. But still the fact remains that the whole field of political economy is much more vast than is usually supposed. The field is, in fact, so great that it is absurd to suppose that one man can cover it all in a lifetime. In but one single branch, that of money, as Professor Jevons says, no economist has ever pretended to have read all the literature. In short, one might properly confine himself, after general training, to the sole study of currency and banking all his life. The reason why the teacher can not do it is plain: it is only within ten or fifteen years that political economy has been allowed a real foothold in our college curriculum; and, if he is not even yet obliged to give tuition also in history and moral philosophy, the instructor is, at least, expected to give a complete knowledge of political economy to a class in three or six months, and add the discussion of ethics, in its proper relation to economics, in, perhaps, another month or two! As yet the necessity for eco-

nomic teaching has been so little recognized
that few chairs exist for instruction in political economy alone; while a proper subdivision
of the work—such as exists in the university
departments of Greek, Chemistry, or Natural
History—would require several chairs, one for
each particular part of the study. Division of
labor has not yet been applied to economic
teaching. But, at least, we can demand that the
economist should not be required to fill the
function of an ethical teacher also. He is inevitably led to it, but it is not in the *rôle* of an economist that he should enter on the new field.

It seems, therefore, necessary to make this
distinction between the work of the economist
and the ethical teacher, if for no other reason
than that, to do one part of his work respecta-
bly well, he should confine himself to that alone.
In fact, many high-sounding programmes exist,
ostensibly covering history, statistics, economics, and social science, which must some day
be remodeled more in accordance with actual
achievements in these fields and the limits of
human life of the few men who are granted to
carry them on.

9

It may now, perhaps, be understood what was meant by saying that ethics begins where political economy leaves off. An illustration will, however, make this meaning more clear. It is an accepted doctrine of political economy that capital is created by saving; and it is shown still further that saving depends upon the "strength of the effective desire to save" in a community. When the process of saving is still further analyzed, it is found that saving means a willingness to abstain from a present use of wealth in consideration of some future, and generally distant, reward. For example, a slave has painfully saved a little money at a time, instead of using it for clothing or amusements, in order to purchase his freedom, even though he does not accomplish it for many years. Political economy does not concern itself with questions of political freedom, for which the slave has a longing. It shows that saving increases in proportion to the ability of a person—no matter for what underlying cause —to bring the future reward so strongly before the mind that it overcomes the pressing, eager, tumultuous demands of the present gratifications; or, in other words, in proportion to the ability to grasp the *unseen* as compared with the *seen.* A familiar illustration of this has been given from the experience of the Jesuits with the natives of Paraguay, over whom they acquired a complete ascendency, and easily managed to get from them labor of the most fatiguing kind; but at evening, when hungry, the *seen* was stronger than the *unseen*, and they uselessly killed their oxen for food, regardless of the coming morrow. In this way political economy has explained the motives which induce men to save, and has shown why the inducement is wanting. And here the duty of the economist ceases. So that, in the case of the slave, political economy does not set itself to explain the force which love of freedom exercises over the human mind, but simply affirms that, if such a force exists, strong enough to overcome a present desire for gratification, it will result in an increase of capital.

But the eager, philanthropic world at once asks, as it considers the condition of the worst of the laboring classes, among whom there is no saving, or thought of the future, How can we induce men to save? For an answer we must not go to the economist, but to the student of ethics. He who has made a study of the mind and character, and knows best their operations, and the springs which lead to action, must set himself to find a solution of the problem—whether it shall be in education, in Christian teaching, or in some form of co-operation and industrial partnership. How the ideals of the laboring classes may be raised is wholly an ethical and not an economic inquiry. There is nothing to prevent an economist from joining in the search; but he is then wearing the uniform of another sovereign. Yet, of course, it is evident that the ethical student can not know where to direct his energies with effect unless he be informed and guided by the work of the economist.

There is, then, a very important connection existing between political economy and the study of practical ethics. And, consequently, to no class in the community does the demand for a knowledge of economic principles, and for a practical realization of the means by which the masses of men should be touched, appeal

with more justice and force than to the educated ministry of the country. Just so far as
they propose to treat social questions in their
work of Christian teaching, or in effective pas-
toral work among the poor, must they learn
what channels political economy has shown to
be open to their leavening efforts. An illustration of this position may be found in the general
question of charities. Political economy has
earnestly taught that reliance upon individual
self-help is more conducive to production than a
necessarily enervating dependence on outside
help, whether it be on the State or on the local
government. It has pointed out the slackening
of restraints on population whenever the State
aided in wages, or in alms-giving. Now, these
principles, so briefly hinted at, have been grossly
violated by those whose good intentions have
proved greater than their wisdom, and who,
under the name of charity, have established institutions for destroying the character and self-
help of the poor. While, on the other hand,
by a movement in direct obedience to economic
principles, the most signal triumph of modern
philanthropy in charitable work has been lately

accomplished by the system of the "Associated
Charities," the object of which has been to assist misfortune through regular visits from persons of discretion, who can supply the lack of
prudence among the unfortunate, but who do
not give money; who find avenues for unused
or dormant powers, teaching the poor what
practical labor they ought to undertake; and
who, by showing how individual effort may be
exercised, remove the existing premiums on
vagrancy, and cease to emasculate exertion by
gifts rendered for no consideration.

There exists between political economy and
Christianity at once a friendly and a close connection; and one is not at variance with the
other. It has been the fashion in the past to
save thinking by applying to political economy
the catch-word "dismal science," because of its
teaching on the question of restraints upon the
increase of population among those classes
whose productive power did not increase cor-
respondingly with their numbers. If political
economy pointed out that an increase of numbers led to misery and poverty in certain conditions, then surely it were practical Christian

teaching to explain this, and strive to prevent this misery and poverty. In fact, the investigator and first expounder of the law of population was a country clergyman in England, Mr. Malthus. In teaching the universal rules of Christian precepts, the minister who expects to be of most good to the poor about him must learn in what practical channels these precepts lead him, or he will be disheartened by dismal failure. But as a Christian teacher, in enforcing the value of the *unseen* over the *seen* he is laying the foundation for the best practical political economy—in fact, the essence of civilization. Such teaching will increase capital and check undue increase of population.

Thus, without going far, we are able to see the laws of Christian ethics working through the medium of practical economic forms. The relation of economic work to the life of the ministry might be further illustrated, but perhaps enough has been said to outline my understanding of it. The student of ethics stands in the very gratifying position of supplementing political economy by suggesting practical means for influencing human nature to better ends.

Political economy rests content with trying to explain the relations between the various phenomena of wealth; while the ethical reformer works to change what is wrong. Political economy explains; it does not judge or reform.

JOURNALISM, although a young profession, is a growing one, and its influence upon public opinion is still greater than that of the ministry. The newspaper has created a new avocation, in which an editor is obliged to deal with all the questions which agitate the human mind. Ideally speaking, the journalist ought to have read well in every subject, especially in home and foreign politics, law, economics, science, ethics, and literature. In practice, a division of labor inevitably takes place. But, even then, some subjects are oftenest before the public for discussion, and this consequently increases the importance of one part of the training for a journalist over another. As has been already pointed out, the largest proportion of questions before Congress are in their nature economic; and to these are to be added the questions of state and local taxation, and

kindred measures, certain to be discussed in
every newspaper which is read. Just here is
the seriousness of the situation. All of these
complex economic questions are sure to be
discussed—irrespective of the knowledge or
preparation of the writer. In other words,
each newspaper is expected by popular opinion to declare itself with proper force and dog-
matism on every subject before the public.
The result of this is, that there is certain to be
some diffusion of ideas on economic questions,
either good or bad, throughout the whole land.
No matter what we think about it, there is sure
to be some teaching of one kind or another.
The important point is, can this teaching be
made good? When we consider the extraordinary power of the press in moulding public
opinion, the responsibility resting on journalists
to give the right economic teaching is almost
deterrent in its seriousness. And since it is
absolutely certain that there will be economic
ideas of some kind in the minds of the public,
it is evident that we can make these ideas good
ones, only by working at the purveyors of such
writing in the journals of the land.

The relation of political economy to journalism is thus seen to be a very different one from that to the ministry. The latter carry out by ethical methods changes suggested by the economist as possible; while the former are economic teachers. In short, careful preparation in political economy is as necessary for an influential writer for the press as it is for the instructor of political economy in the schools and colleges. The day, we hope, is fast passing when a teacher of economics can face a class, without previous training and study; and it is quite as absurd to place a man in an editor's chair who is distinctly unqualified for his position in respect of an adequate power to discuss economic questions.

It would seem desirable, after a general course which gives a *coup d'œil* of the whole field, that the journalist should, if his time is somewhat limited, give himself to studying the present economic questions on which political issues are turning, or which are uppermost in men's minds. Such a course of reading must necessarily change with the movement of events, but a few hints as to useful books might not be·out of place. The subjects which are now before us have been already mentioned (Chapter I), but, besides a general control of economic principles, a knowledge of the following subjects, at least, should be urged as absolutely necessary for a journalist's immediate equipment:

1. The History of American Tariffs;
2. The National Banking System;
3. The Theory and History of Bimetallism;
4. American Shipping; and
5. Taxation.

The question might be naturally asked, How can this preparation be obtained? To those who have the means of acquiring a university education the answer is evident. Another class, composed of those hard-working, self-educated men, who are often doing excellent work without the prestige of a college training, can now enter the university courses as special students, pursuing only particular studies, of their own choosing. But, for the large class of men who can not now leave their stations, and yet would gladly improve their daily opportunities for study, something can be done to make their work easier through the means of bibliographies issued by libraries and specialists. These should be graded: some lists of books should be adapted to a class not accustomed to technical work; and then a complete and minute bibliography for specialists should be added. The scholars and universities owe a debt to the community which has supplied them with the endowments and resources for carrying on instruction, and by the publication of helpful bibliographies can well afford to render the great accumulations of books, and the skill which they have gained through special studies, useful to the less fortunate. Such lists are the campaign maps of any subject, which, in these days of many books, is obscured merely by the multiplicity of publications.

As a practical illustration of the feasibleness of this plan, it is easy to show what can be done in the above-mentioned subjects which were considered necessary to a journalist's efficiency.

1. *The History of American Tariffs.*

A bibliography of a general character has been already made * under the following heads:

a. General works.

b. Earlier Periods.

c. Noteworthy Documents.

d. Pauper-Labor Argument.

e. View of Early Manufactures.

f. Later View of Manufactures.

g. Present Tariff (1884).

2. *The National Banking System.*

Inasmuch as, to my knowledge, no bibliography exists on this topic, I shall make some suggestions as to books.

"Extracts from the Laws of the United States relating to Currency and Finance" (Sever, Cambridge) gives the National Bank Act in connection with other financial legislation in a brief form.

"The National Bank Act" is published separately by the Government (and also by the Homans Publishing Co., 251 Broadway, New York).

---

* In an abridgment of Mill's "Political Economy," by the author (D. Appleton & Co., 1884, second ed. 1885), pp. 631–633.

"Reports of the Comptroller of the Currency," are published annually in December, by the Government in separate form, and also in the Finance Reports with other documents. The Comptroller is the officer who supervises the national banks, and makes his reports to the Secretary of the Treasury. They contain official information as to banking statistics, and all questions affecting the condition of the banks. They do not begin, of course, before 1864. Those under the tenure of John Jay Knox are especially good.

" The Decisions of the United States Courts " on the Banking Laws can be found analyzed in the Comptroller's Reports (e. g., in that of 1884, p. 77).

" Finance Report of 1861 " gives the first recommendations to Congress, by Secretary Chase, for the adoption of the system. See also his Report for 1862.

"Comptroller's Report of 1875" contains a history and explanation of the national banking scheme. See also Report for 1876.

Bowen's " American Political Economy," chap. xvi, discusses the value of the plan.

"The Advantages of the National Bank System of the United States now in Force," in the "Banker's Magazine," March, 1868, by George Walker. Also published separately.

Some general treatment in modest form may be found in M. L. Scudder's "National Banking: a Discussion of the Merits of the Present System" (1879); and H. W. Richardson's "National Banks" (New York, 1880).

As to the machinery for the retirement of notes, see a discussion in the "Atlantic Monthly," February, 1882, "The Refunding Bill of 1881."

3. *The Theory and History of Bimetallism.*

A bibliography * has already been compiled under the following heads:

a. Standards of Value.

b. Bimetallic Theory.

c. Gresham's Law.

d. Compensatory Effect of Two Standards.

e. Effect of Law on the Relative Values of Gold and Silver.

* In the abridgment of Mill's "Political Economy," already referred to, pp. 633–635.

f. Production, and Relative Values, of Gold and Silver.

g. Demonetization of Silver by Germany.

h. Latin Union.

i. Flow of Silver to the East.

j. Depreciation of Silver.

k. Appreciation of Gold.

l. Bimetallism in the United States.

4. *American Shipping.*

A bibliography * has likewise been prepared on the following topics:

a. English Navigation Acts.

b. Navigation Laws of the United States.

c. Growth of American Shipping.

d. Steam and Iron Ships.

e. Decline of American Shipping.

f. Burdens on Ship-owners.

5. *Taxation.*

A few suggestions as to sources of information will aid an energetic student to get a general view of the subject.

E. De Parieu's " Traité des impôts consi-

---

* Abridgment of Mill's " Political Economy," pp. 635, 636.

dérés sous le rapport historique, economique, et politique en France et à l'étranger" (second edition, 1867), 4 vols. This gives a comparison of the system of taxation in various countries.

Alexander Johnstone Wilson's "The National Debts, Taxes, and Rates." (London, 1882, in "Citizens Series.") This furnishes a view of the whole English system of taxation in a small compass.

R. Dudley Baxter's "The Taxation of the United Kingdom" (1869) offers explanations of the incidence of taxation on the various classes in the community. See also the same writer's "National Debts" (1871).

"Report of the Commissioners appointed to revise the Laws for the Assessment and Collection of Taxes," to the New York Legislature (Albany, 1875), by David A. Wells, Edwin Dodge, George W. Cuyler.

Second Report, by the same authors, with a code of laws relating to Assessment and Taxation (1872). These are two notable reports.

"Report of the Commissioners appointed to inquire into the Expediency of revising and amending the Laws relating to Taxation and Exemption therefrom." Made to the Massachusetts Lower House (Doc. No. 15), January 1875.

William Minot's "Taxation" (1881) discusses the wrongs of double taxation. See also "Social Science Journal," January, 1878, for a better treatment of the same subject by the same writer.

CHAPTER V.

METHODS OF TEACHING POLITICAL ECONOMY.

A NATION is sometimes so bitterly taught by sad experience in financial errors—as was the case with France in John Law's time, and again in the issue of paper assignats during the Revolution—that, on the principle of the " burned child," it afterwards finds that it unconsciously keeps to the right and avoids the wrong path. So that to-day France is a country where correct conceptions of money are almost universal, and whose public monetary experiments are, as a rule, most admirably conducted. In somewhat the same way does the individual gain his proper knowledge of political economy. Principles must be seen working in a concrete form. The key to efficient teaching of it is to connect principles with actual facts; and this process can go on in the beginner's mind only through experience. By experience, I mean the personal (subjective) effort of each one to realize the working of the principle for himself in the facts of his own knowledge. The pupil must be put in the way of assimilating for himself the principles of his subject in such a manner that he feels their truth because they are apparent in explanation of concrete things all around him. That this is the aim to be always kept in view by the teacher and student has been made clear, it is to be hoped, by the previous analysis of the character and discipline of political economy in Chapters II and III. It is now my purpose to make some suggestions as to the practical methods of teaching by which this can be carried into effect.

1. The relative advantages of lectures and recitations for political economy have never, to my knowledge, been openly discussed. An experience with both methods of teaching leads me to think that the lecture system, pure and simple, is so ineffective that it ought to be set aside at once as entirely undesirable. The disciplinary power to be gained by the study is almost wholly lost to the student by this method of teaching. Nothing is so useful as a sharp

struggle, an effort, a keen discussion, or possibly a failure of comprehension at the time; for nothing will so awaken one to intellectual effort, and finally result in the safe lodgment of the principle within one's mind as an obstruction and its removal. This is not gained by listening to lectures. No matter how clear the exposition of the principles may be, no matter how fresh and striking the illustrations, it still remains that the student is relieved by the instructor from carrying on the mental processes which he ought to conduct for himself. In fact, the clearer the exposition by the instructor, the less is left to the student—the lecturer, in fact, is the chief gainer by the system. Moreover, while listening to a connected and logical unfolding of the principles, the student is lulled into a false belief that, as he understands all that has been so clearly presented to him, he knows the subject quite well enough; and the result is to send out a number of conceited men who really can not carry on a rational economic discussion. They wholly miss the discipline which gives exactitude, mental breadth, keenness, and power to express

.themselves plainly and to the point. Then, not being forced to think over a principle in its application to various phases of concrete phenomena, they know the truth only in connection with the illustrations given by the lecturer, while they utterly fail to assimilate the principles into their own thinking. The subject then becomes to them a matter of memory. They memorize the general statements without ever realizing their practical side, and that which is memorized for the day of examination is forgotten more speedily than it is learned, and the sum total of the discipline has been simply a stretching of the memory. In fact, with the average student, in almost any subject the lecture system leads to cramming. At the best, it affords a constant temptation to put off that kind of mental struggle which ought to be carried on by by the student himself—a period of doubts and questions—by which alone a clearer conception of the subject ultimately emerges. In fact, without it, it is doubtful if the student ever gets much, if any, of that mental attrition on the subject which is the most valuable part of the work. An experience of a year with

lecturing in an elementary course to a class of
two hundred and fifty, including the best and
the poorest men in the university, practically
convinced me, when taken with other evidence,
of the truth of the above position; for, as con-
trasted with the work of similar men in other
years under a different system, their examination-books were the most unsatisfactory I had
ever read.

The usual alternative to the lecture system
is the plan of recitations from a text-book.
Even the simplest form of recitations is, in my
opinion, better than listening to lectures. At
the very least, the student is put to it to express the sense in his own words, and that,
too, under the criticism of the teacher. But
this plan has its evident difficulties. If the
pupil is called upon for only that which is con-
tained in the book, he falls into the habit of
memorizing, and fails to think for himself. If
you give him the clew, he can tell you on what
part of the page the statement is found, and he
can talk in the language of the book; but he
knows nothing of the power of applying it to
what he sees. If the learner is very clever and

inquisitive, he may do something for himself, but the average pupil quite misses the real good of such a course.

2. As it is evident that neither lectures nor formal recitations in the old fashion are satisfactory, we are inevitably led to adopt a plan which possesses the advantages of both. Some text-book is essential as a basis for the instruction.* In it the pupil should find an exposition of the principles, and a provocation to apply them to practical things as he reads. Then he should come to the class-room as intelligently familiar with the principles as his reading can make him. Now comes the work of the instructor. With a class of beginners, it is sur-

---

* The question naturally arises in the teacher's mind, What is the best text-book? This, of course, is a matter of individual experience and judgment, and competent persons will differ in offering advice. From my own point of view, I should strongly recommend for mature students, who can give to it fifty or sixty hours of recitation, Mill's "Principles of Political Economy." For those who wish a less severe course, for a shorter time, Mr. and Mrs. Marshall's "Economies of Industry" is an excellent book. For the same persons, a forthcoming book by Professor Simon Newcomb, to be published this summer (1885), would be admirable. I have seen the advanced sheets, and find the system of applying principles to facts at the end of each chapter admirably carried out. For books to be consulted by the teacher, he is referred to the "Library" list at the beginning of this volume.

prising how easy it is to show even to the best men a gap in their knowledge, or a misunderstanding of the principle. Present an illustration different from that of the book, and ask them to explain the situation, and very few will be able to respond. The necessity of seeing the essential point in the facts and the attempt to describe the operation of the principle will effectually rout the man who has merely memorized the book, and teach him to think out the matter more thoroughly for himself in the future. The teacher, also, will try to find out the accidental obstacles which in a young mind obstruct the understanding of the point in question. Let the pupil be asked to state the matter, and let the teacher note the imperfections. At the same time he can stimulate another student by questioning him as to one of these imperfections. If a correction is not obtained in a clear and connected manner from a member of the class, let the instructor apply the Socratic method. At first ask a question which the learner readily understands, and then lead him naturally and gradually by logical steps up to the point wherein he had failed of understanding.   He will then see his own difficulty, and at the same time he has had a little robust exercise for his mind.   If this is carried on before his fellows, it will the better cultivate coolness and self-control before an audience.

3. Above all, the hour should not be wasted in simply rehearsing what has been read in the book.   The student should go away from the class-room feeling that he has received some new idea, or some interesting fact which illustrates his subject.   The work of the class-room should be cumulative in its effect as compared with the results of text-book reading.   The teacher should in every way stimulate questions from members of his class, and urge the statement by them, either orally or in writing, of their doubts and difficulties.   If there is some timidity in presenting a weakness in the presence of a class, ask a question of some more manly person of the number, and the timid student will soon see that others are not much better off than he.   In fact, all will have difficulties in understanding, or in interpreting principles, some trivial, some serious; and the pupil will become discouraged unless these are removed.

When each one sees that others are also hindered by obstacles, there will be a greater freedom in asking questions. Moreover, in order to keep up a steady and regular training, which will produce the best disciplinary results, let the questions of the instructor every day run backward in review, and especially aim to bring out the connection of one part of the subject with another. It will be very effective if done just about the time that the past work is growing a little dim before the presence of newer ideas. In no subject, perhaps, more than, in political economy, is it necessary to know the preliminary steps in order to understand the later work; so that the pupil must be actually in possession of principles previously expounded, for which he may be called upon at any time. It is simply impossible for a person to be absent and neglectful for a time in his study, and then come into the class-room to make a brilliant show on an intermediate fragment of the subject. He can be too easily exposed as a humbug to attempt it a second time. Moreover, thus to force him to do the work as he goes along is the greatest favor one can do for the pupil ; and the usual cramming before the examination becomes, in reality, a general review, which is very useful in bringing him to see the connection existing throughout the whole subject.

4. If the class is so large that it is impossible for the instructor to reach each member as often as he might wish with the above method, there is one device which is more or less useful. At the beginning of the hour let him write a question upon the blackboard, to be answered by each one in writing within the first ten or fifteen minutes. The attempt to write out an explanation clearly, without hint or clew from the instructor, will reveal to the best student the deficiencies and gaps in his knowledge. Each one will then have the keenest interest to know what is considered a satisfactory answer to the question. At the next exercise of the class, the instructor can read some good and some bad answers, point out the general mistakes, and advise his pupils for the future. No exercise can be better than this in cultivating the habit of careful expression, and in learning how to make a clear and pointed exposition of

a subject in a short space. This practice tends to secure the accuracy which in the oral discussions is made second to fluency and readiness. The teacher, I believe, will be forced to some such method as this, if he hopes to get a real idea of the prevailing difficulties in the minds of his class. They are in the nature of anonymous communications, in which, as no one else can know what he is writing, the student may without timidity show exactly what he can do. In fact, the written answers afford admirable means of judging how far the class have taken serious hold of the subject, and they enable the instructor to modify the nature of his questions to members, or to change the character of the exercise to suit a set of slower men. But one of the best uses of these written answers, in my experience, has been to break down the timidity which prevented questions in the classroom. The criticism of an answer before the class is certain to bring out as defender, either the writer, or one who gave a similar reply; and the whole number of men will be very restive under criticism of a piece of work at which each has tried his hand. As soon as questioning becomes natural and easy, the number of written exercises can be diminished, and the whole hour given to discussions with the class.

5. Since the chief work of the class-room is not to enable students to discover principles, but rather to understand and apply them, probably the most useful method of interesting a class is to present to them, in extracts from the newspapers of the day, bits of fallacious discussions * which may come under the head of the subject in hand, and then to ask for criticism and discussion. This will also suggest doubts and difficulties which had not been anticipated in the minds of some, and will aid in stimulating questions. The appositeness of a timely topic before the public is peculiarly serviceable for such purposes. In fact, the practical matters of our own country will never fail to excite a lively interest in almost any class; and through this interest the teacher can find a

---

* Professor W. G. Sumner has published a volume of "Problems in Political Economy" (1884), which adopts the plan above described for advanced classes. The system is also most excellently carried out in a forthcoming elementary treatise on Political Economy by Simon Newcomb, to be published during the coming summer.

way of leading men to study principles more carefully. A National or State campaign is very likely to furnish an instructor with a plentiful supply of extracts from speeches of an economic character for discussion by his class. The learner in political economy is not hindered by the same disagreeable obstacles, as hamper the medical student, in finding subjects on which to put his learning into practice.

6. Many minds are unable to keep hold on an abstraction, or general principle; or they may have been untrained in making nice distinctions between ideas or definitions. And these students form a very large proportion of the ordinary classes. To such persons a skillful teacher ought to offer some help. Diagrams have seemed to me most useful for this purpose, and a reason can be given for their use. Just as in beginning a strange language, when words of widely different meaning have a similarity to the untutored eye, the distinctions do not make much impression. So it is in regard to principles and definitions in political economy. Therefore, visible expression of the abstract relationships, by diagrams, or by any figures

which represent the abstract in a concrete form, will be of very considerable service to the average student. This matter seems to me to be of such practical importance in teaching that it will be worth while to illustrate my meaning by a few examples.

(*a.*) Since material wealth comprises all things that have value ; since capital is only that wealth employed in reproduction, and not used by the owner himself ; and since money is that part of wealth in circulation aiding in the transfer of goods — the relations between the three may be expressed to the commonest apprehension by some such device as the following, in which the area of circle A represents the total amount of wealth ; B, the capital saved out of the total wealth ; and C, the money by which goods are transferred—only that part of circle C being capital which, inside of circle B, is being used as a means to production.

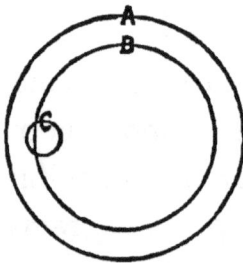

Again, (*b*) it is seen that different classes of laborers, arranged according to their skill,

form, as it were, social strata, of which the
largest and the poorest paid is composed of
the unskilled laborers at the bottom. This
may be shown to the eye at once by the sec-
tion of a triangle, in which A represents the
largest and least paid class; B, the better-edu-
cated, and relatively more skillful laborers;
ending finally in the few at the top, of the most

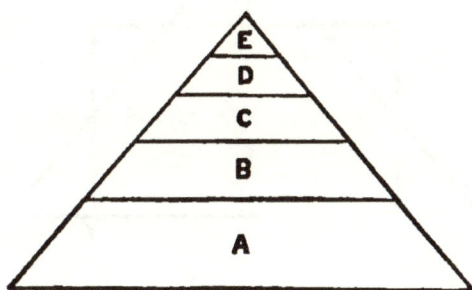

competent executive managers. Now, if A
were to become as fully skilled as B, and competition should become free between all members of A and B; and if this were to go on in
the same way to include C—the effects of this
breaking down of the barriers which hinder
competition might be illustrated by the following changes in the above triangle: the areas
of A, B, and C may be thrown together into

one area within the whole of which movement and choice are perfectly free to the laborer, and wherein wages are in proportion to sacrifice. This can be done by striking out the lines of division between A, B, and C, and representing the change by the area included between the base and the dotted lines.

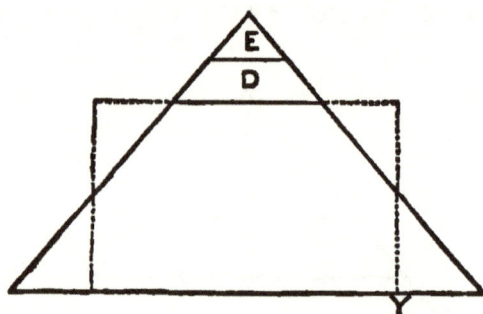

Examples might be multiplied in illustration of my method, but these must suffice. By such means there can be planted inside even the dull mind an outline of an idea which can then be modeled and shaded to the condition of a natural truth. The teacher will find, by experience, that an idea thus given is very seldom forgotten. The pupil has thus once turned the abstraction into a concrete form, and, after he has once grasped it, he can now use it for himself. It does not at all imply that he will get hard and definite conceptions of human affairs by this process; for he is shown that the principle appears in other forms, and he is constantly seeing that it is so. Having found out how a principle explains one set of facts, he can be led to see its application to other conditions.

7. In close connection with this method, but having an entirely different end in view, is the use of charts and graphic representations of statistics. The method just described above aimed to help in finding concrete expressions for the general principles; but graphic methods usually serve best to assist in that part of the economic process heretofore referred to as verification. There is an abundance of economic facts in regard to which the connection between cause and effect is either unknown or grossly misunderstood. In truth, the subjects to which political economy applies are constantly changing, nay, are even multiplying. These data, after having been collected with great care (which is the duty of the statistician), are the materials for the process

of verification. By this "systematized method of observation," says Cairnes,* "we can most effectually check and verify the accuracy of our reasoning from the fundamental assumptions of the science; while the same expedient offers, also, by much the most efficacious means of bringing into view the action of those minor or disturbing agencies which modify, sometimes so extensively, the actual course of events. The mode in which these latter influences affect the phenomena of wealth is, in general, unobvious, and often intricate, so that their existence does not readily discover itself to a reasoner engaged in the development of the more capital economic doctrines." In this part of the process graphic representations of statistics are invaluable.

Every one knows the common dislike of dreary statistics; to many persons columns of statistics are repellent or meaningless. Collections of facts regarding banking, finance, taxation, and wages become a tangle in which one's direction is constantly lost. But arranged graphically the whole direction of a movement

* "Logical Method," p. 97.

is seen at once, and the mind takes in new and unexpected changes, which force an investigation into their cause. Moreover, there comes a certain breadth of treatment, when, in looking at the facts graphically expressed, one is able to see the whole field at once. There is no waste of thought on temporary and accidental movements, for the action is seen from beginning to end at one glance. There are many charts which would illustrate this meaning very distinctly; but perhaps none are simpler than the one here appended, showing the steady and continuous fall in the value of silver relatively to gold since the discovery of the New World. No one has ever claimed that there has been any "unfriendliness" displayed toward silver in the legislation of the chief countries of the world before the present century, at the farthest, and yet the white metal has been steadily on the decline ever since the Spanish galleons, in the fifteenth century, began to pour the precious metals of America into the coffers of Spain.

Another illustration of my meaning can be found in the study of the facts relating to

12

Chart showing the Changes in the Relative Values of Gold and Silver from 1501 to 1880.

From 1501 to 1680 a space is allotted to each twenty years ; from 1681 to 1871, to each ten years ; from 1876 to 1880, to each year.

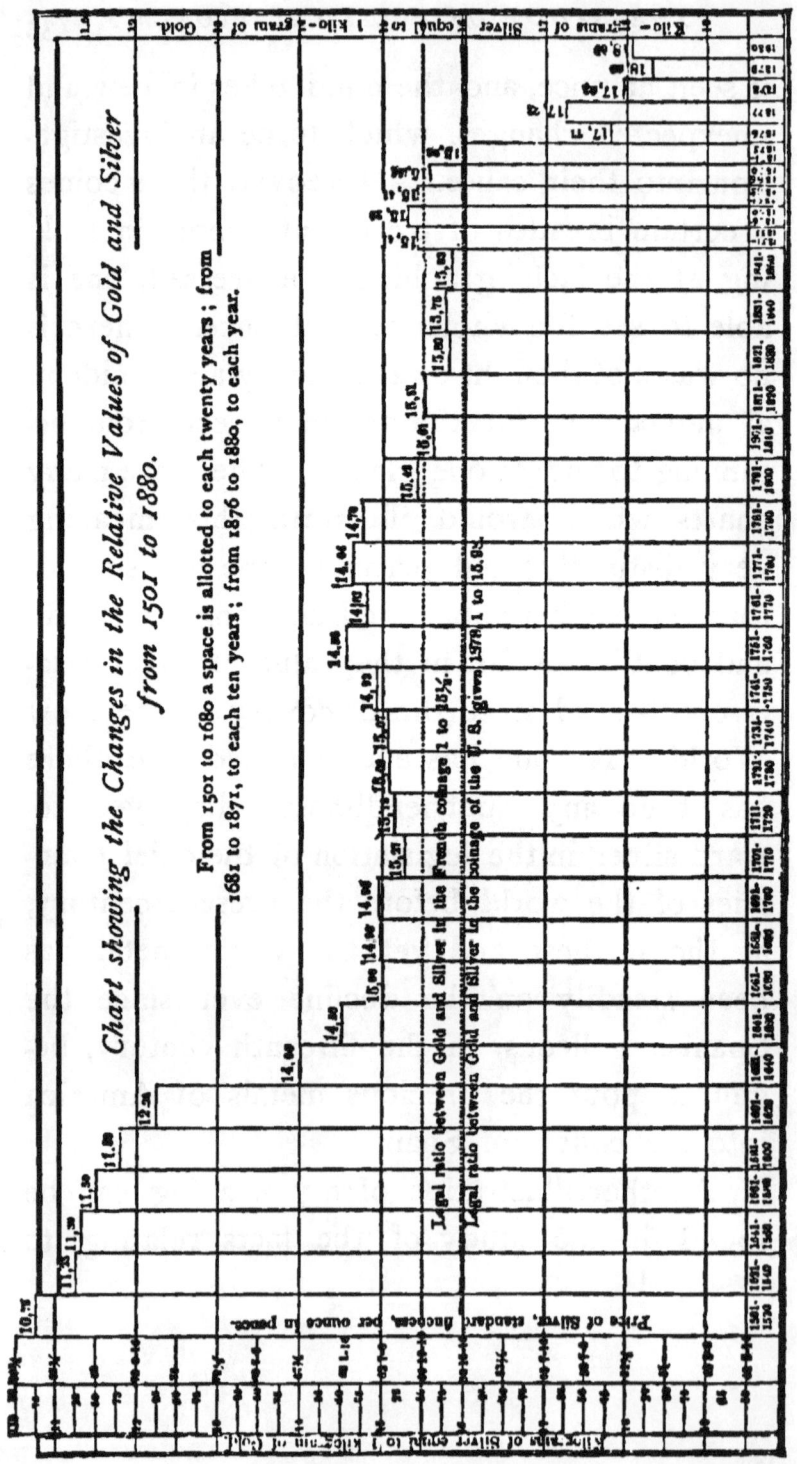

Legal ratio between Gold and Silver in the French coinage 1 to 15½.

Legal ratio between Gold and Silver in the coinage of the U. S. given 1978? 1 to 15.92.

Price of Silver, standard, £nceace, per ounce in pence.

Kilo = Grains of ⚬ Silver ⚬ equal to ⚬ 1 Kilo = ⚬ Grain of ⚬ Gold.

Kilo = Grains of ⚬ Silver ⚬ equal to ⚬ 1 Kilo = ⚬ Grain of ⚬ Gold.

Kilogram of Silver equal to 1 kilogram of Gold.

American shipping. We have heard—until
the story is now worn threadbare—of the decline of our tonnage engaged in the foreign
carrying trade; we have listened to explanations which attribute this decline wholly to
our Civil War, or to the introduction of steam
and iron (or steel) ships. But by collating the
statistics for sailing-vessels alone, if we separate the question entirely from steam and iron,
and compare our situation in regard to sailing-
vessels with that before the use of steam—
the period of our great shipping prosperity—
the comparison gives some· curious results.
These are shown to the eye at a glance; and
it would have been difficult to find them had
not this graphic system been applied. The
striking facts imperatively call for explanation.
We see at once that, practically, to the end of
the war our sailing tonnage changed only with
the total; and that after 1869 it was the foreign tonnage which then rose and kept a close
attendance on the total, while the American
figures showed scarcely any relative change.
The two lines, representing foreign and American vessels, after a short struggle with each

Chart showing the Tonnage of Sailing Vessels entered at Seaports of the United States each year, from 1844 to 1883, inclusive.

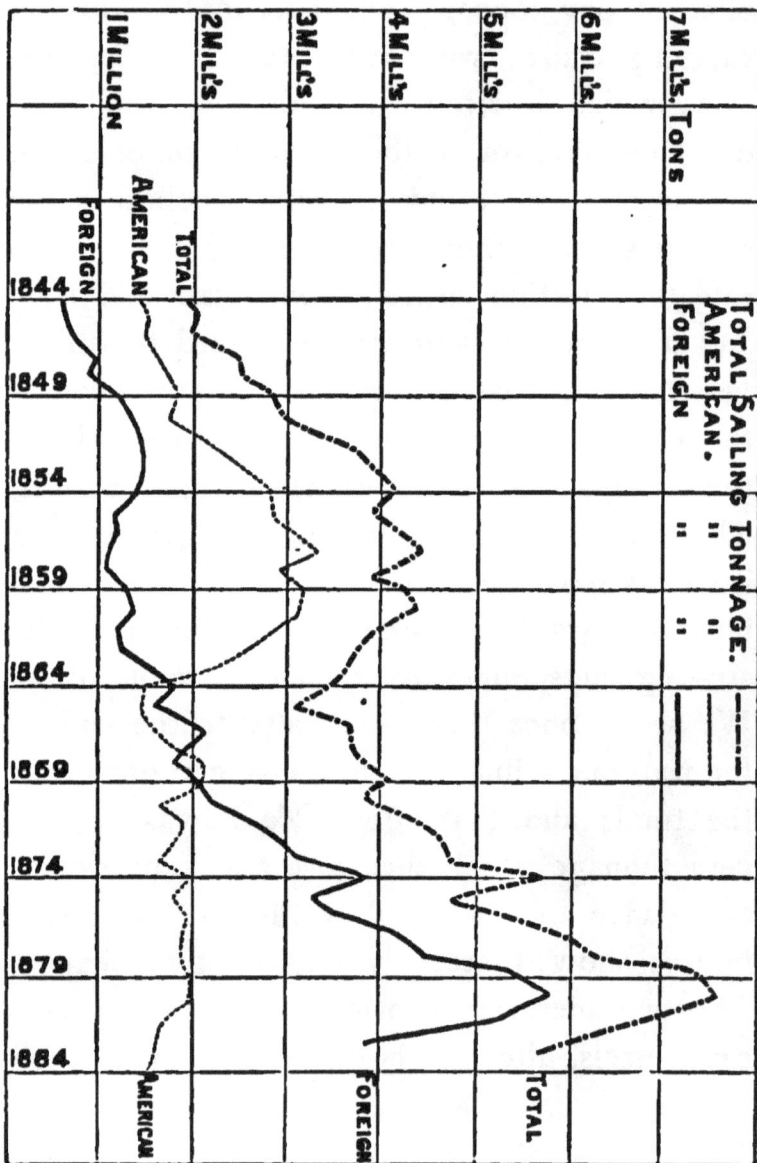

other exactly changed their relative positions
to the line representing the total tonnage. The
graphic method lays bare the naked facts for
the scalpel of the investigator. The student is
then in a position to apply principles and discover explanations. No table of figures, I am
convinced, would disclose vital relations in the
statistics in the searching way by which it is
done with the aid of a few lines on a chart.

In short, the more extended collection of
economic data is now rendered possible through
the better methods employed in census and
statistical bureaus, and the resort to the work
of verification of economic principles in the
examination of these data is one of the best
means by which political economy can be redeemed from the baseless and common charge
of being made up of formulæ which have no
practical use. Into this work one can carry no
instrument so effective and helpful as graphic
representations. In fact, the investigator, after
having collected his tables and columns of figures, will find his gain in first putting them
in some graphic form, before he can intelligently see exactly with what he has to grapple;

then he can turn his energies directly upon the problems which are disclosed by the chart to every other eye as well as his own.

There are, however, other important gains to be derived from the use of charts by the teacher. Above all, they are interesting. They will attract the idler by something new which he can easily understand, although he can not explain the causes; they stimulate the quick by putting them at once in possession of the facts to be explained. When lecturing upon practical questions, one great difficulty presents itself to the teacher in trying to find the means of laying before his class the actual condition of the subject which is to be investigated. If it were proposed to place the statistics on the blackboard before him, the time of the lecturer would all be lost while the student was copying figures. The references to the books can be given where these figures dealt with by the lecturer are collected, but by a chart long columns of statistics are easily imported into the class-room, become the basis of discussion, and are photographed on the listener's mind once for all in an attractive and interesting way. The slow and painful work of months is in this way presented to a class in a few minutes, and the practical lessons caught at a glance. For this purpose, charts are the labor-saving machines of statistics.

A word or two as to the details of preparing charts may not be impertinent. They can be made on common glazed white cotton cloth (called sarcenet cambric), which receives ink or water-colors; but the labor of ruling the cloth in squares before the construction of the chart is very considerable. Use can be made, however, of heavy manila paper, made large enough by sticking two large sheets together. Some printers can now rule this paper in squares to suit the convenience of the worker; but these guiding-lines ought to be faint, and not so heavy as to overpower the lines of the chart. The instructor can also have a blackboard ruled with faint white lines, after the manner of co-ordinate paper, in his room, on which he can in half an hour put a simple chart, ready for the coming lecture. Different colored crayons serve the purpose admirably. Students can then use co-ordinate paper in their notes, and draw off an accurate copy of the chart in a few moments, before or after the lecture. This is a necessary course, unless some more feasible method than now exists should be found by the instructor for multiplying copies from his single chart in such numbers as to supply all members of his class.

So far I have been speaking of charts for the class-room. Perhaps, in their own good time, such economic charts can be bought of educational agencies. But ordinary co-ordinate paper, on a small scale, is the best form in which first to construct the chart. It can be purchased in sheets at a small price, and is invaluable for both student and instructor. In fact, no lesson is more stimulating to a class than to give them the data of a subject and ask them to put it into graphic form with the use of such paper. For the first time they begin to realize that statistics are not dry; indeed, any one who has turned over the pages of Walker's "Statistical Atlas" will find out for himself how the columns of census tables* can

---

* Another successful attempt, on an elaborate scale, has been made with the materials of the census of 1880 by Messrs. Gannett

talk to him in forms and colors not only without weariness, but with a sense of surprise at the interest they excite.

8. When the instructor comes to examinations he will find some difficulties in combining an ideal plan with actual conditions. In making out a paper he ought, of course, to keep in view that the questions should be selected so as to test not the memory, but the power of the pupil to apply principles. For this reason the ideal paper should contain nothing which the student has seen in that form before. The facts he is called upon to explain ought to be fresh ones, and the fallacies he is to examine should be such as he had not previously considered. This, however, is not wholly necessary. The explanation of parts of the subject is certain to be difficult enough to warrant questions upon them even if they have been referred to in the class-room many times before. For practical purposes, however, it seems best to remember that a class is composed of all kinds of persons, and, while the majority of

and Hewes in Scribner's " Statistical Atlas of the United States " (1885).

the questions should be of the character which I have described, yet at least a few easier and more encouraging questions should be set. In the examination-room the student, moreover, should be instructed to study each question with care, and avoid haste in answering, before he is sure that he has really caught the pivotal point of the question. Fairly good students often write about the question but do not answer it. It should be definitely understood that no credit is to be given for irrelevant answers. Then, also, the examination can be used as a teaching process; since, by inserting an important subject, the attention given to it at these times will be such as to keep it from speedy oblivion. Moreover, it will be well, as soon after the examination as possible, to read a good and a poor answer to each question before the class. They will know better what is expected of them in the future—like troops after their first fight. After such an examination the instructor will find his class much more disciplined and more ready to exert themselves in the intellectual wrestling. The vigorous preparation for the examination has really given them a better grasp of the subject, and the teacher can easily bring on a warm discussion now, because they really know something and feel that they know it. In all this it is understood, of course, that I have had in mind written examinations.

9. When first approaching the study, it has been found to be of service to some minds to suggest that on the first reading of the text-book they note in the margins in a few penciled words the gist of each paragraph as it is read; then, at the close of the chapter, that the reader review it by means of his marginal notes, and, finally, make a general but brief synopsis of the chapter. This will both save time and teach that essential thing—how to study rapidly but thoroughly. It will destroy aimless reading, which is so common in these days of many books.

10. Inasmuch as a vigorous contact of mind with mind on a subject which students are approaching for the first time is necessary to produce something more than a cartilaginous or veal-like quality in their knowledge, it is desirable to stimulate discussion among members of

the class outside of the class-room. To accomplish this purpose, I know of no better plan than to recommend students to form temporary clubs of three or four persons to meet two or three times a week for an hour's discussion of the questions and topics which have been suggested by the text-book, by newspapers, or by facts of every-day observation. Such discussions, if the evil of irrelevancy can be frowned upon, will toughen the intellectual fiber, and give the means also of getting more from the instructor through questions upon difficulties and disagreements which have arisen in the clubs.* Congenial persons might group themselves together in this way with profit to their economic progress, and gain something also in social pleasure of a healthy kind.

11. In advanced courses, much of what has been said in regard to details in the conduct of

---

* When about twenty, John Stuart Mill met twice a week in Threadneedle Street, from 8.30 to 10 A. M., with a political economy club, composed of Grote, Roebuck, Ellis, Graham, and Prescott, in which they discussed James Mill's and Ricardo's books. It was understood that a topic should not be passed by until each member had had full chance for a discussion of his difficulties and objections. In these meetings Mill elaborated whatever he has added to the knowledge of political economy.

the class will be less important, because the teaching is necessarily different in kind. Such courses naturally fall either (1) into those which continue to study principles, as in the systems of various writers or schools of political economy in the past and present, or (2) into those which treat historical or practical questions. In the former, the lecture system is unsatisfactory for reasons already given; for the members of the class should themselves be constantly wrestling with the fuller discussion of subjects in which they can hitherto have had only a general knowledge. Experience seems to show that a topic, furnished with references to writers, affords the best method of procedure. This, of course, implies a good working library and a list of reserved books.

In the practical courses a large part of the training consists in teaching the student how to use books, how to familiarize himself with the principal storehouses of statistics, such as the English " Parliamentary Documents," or our own Government publications; how to collect his materials in a useful form; how to apply graphic representations wherever possible; in
13

brief, to learn how to carry on an investigation in the economic field. Of course, the familiarity with the facts of several of the leading questions of the day will form no small part of the advantage of such work. But the greatest good comes, of course, from putting the student on his own resources at once and forcing him to find his own materials, look up his own books and authorities, and come to a conclusion on the subject assigned to him independently of all aid or suggestion. The instructor can then at the conferences take up a paper for criticism and discussion, or.first assign it to another member for that purpose. This is a feasible plan; but, if carried on throughout a whole course, it requires of the student in a regular college course so much time that his other work must suffer, and, in addition, but few subjects can be taken up in this thorough and leisurely way. This plan can be properly carried out only when there are a few persons able to devote their whole time to some economic investigations. In practice it has been found best to use the lecture system partially. One subject can be taken up by the instructor at regular exercises, for which he furnishes beforehand the references, and partly lectures and partly discusses the subject with his class, thus guiding them steadily over the field and directing the disposition of the time to be devoted to each subject. In this way many more subjects can be reached during the year. But the advantages of the investigating method can be partly retained by requiring a monograph from each member of the class on a practical subject of his own selection from a list prepared by the instructor, and this thesis can count for attendance on part of the lecture-work. In this thesis the student is pushed to do his best to give a really serious study to some particular topic, and he is expected to do it independently of any aid beyond general oversight and direction; and he is warned that the paper will be of greater value, provided it contains the bibliography of the subject and constant reference by page and volume to his authorities.

12. The preparation of bibliographies is part of a teacher's duty. Moreover, he who has access to a rich and well-appointed library can do a service to the rest of his guild by leaving be-

hind him notes of his bookish experiences. He can in a few words say whether a book is good or bad for a particular use, or indicate what part of it contains a valuable discussion or useful facts in a subject within his study. For this purpose it has been a great convenience to have little blank-books of ordinary stiff manila paper, six inches by three, with each sheet perforated like postage-stamps near the butt of the book, so that it can be torn off smoothly. On each page a book can be entered under a suitable heading, with its exact title and author, and room still be left for a very generous amount of criticism or commendation, or for noting the contents of the book. The cards can be laid away alphabetically by subjects in a drawer, and will prove of invaluable aid at many times. Books of which one has heard but never seen, can also be entered with a star, to be erased when a book has been examined. This systematic habit is peculiarly desirable when one is hunting for the facts of a certain subject. By this means one will be saved the loss of time caused by failure to remember where a statement has once been seen.

13. In the foregoing remarks on methods of teaching political economy, I have kept in mind persons of the age and maturity possessed by usual college students. As a rule, these are the only persons who are given instruction in this subject. Still, knowing as we do the need of simple elementary instruction in political economy in the secondary and high schools, so that younger pupils of less maturity than the college student ought to have good effective teaching, something ought to be said as to the methods which may be serviceable for such classes.

A difficulty with which we are met at the outset is the lack of training among high-school teachers for original and suggestive object-teaching in economics. Any scheme, based on such a system, implies. the possession of a very considerable economic training by the teachers. What is meant may be seen by the following excellent suggestions for certain parts of the study made by Dr. Ely:*

"The writer has indeed found it possible to

* In "Methods of Teaching and Studying History," edited by G. Stanley Hall, p. 63.

entertain a school-room full of boys, varying in age from five to sixteen, with a discourse on two definitions of capital—one taken from a celebrated writer, and the other from an obscure pamphlet on socialism by a radical reformer. As the school was in the country, illustrations were taken from farm-life, such as corn-planting and harvesting, and from the outdoor sports of the boys, such as trapping for rabbits."

In teaching the functions of money, the following approach to the subject; suggested by the same writer as a means of awakening an interest, is a good one: "Take into the classroom the different kinds of money in use in the United States, both paper and coin, and ask questions about them, and talk about them. Show the class a greenback and a national banknote, and ask them to tell you the difference. After they have all failed, as they probably will, ask some one to read what is engraved on the notes, after which the difference may be further elucidated."

If the teacher is sufficiently master of the subject to proceed by such ways to acquire a

hold on the young pupil he will probably not—
as things now go—be found in a high school.
It is to be hoped that he may in the future;
but, until that is the fact, some more practicable
method of teaching must be adopted.   Much
must, therefore, depend on the text-book.   But
no fully satisfactory one is available for such
purposes.   Of existing books the following may
be suggested: W. S. Jevons's "Primer of Political Economy" (1878).   This little treatise is
marred by the treatment of utility and value;
but yet it is a really good sketch of the subject
in 134 pages.   The teacher can further illustrate the principles to his class by familiar facts,
as already explained.   The instructor should set
forth distinctly in his mind, as a general object
to be kept before him, the attempt to leave in
the understanding of his pupils some simple
principle in each case.   If he is talking of capital, the several illustrations should all lead the
pupil back to the essential truth which is finally
to be stated in general terms.   Then, the pupil,
when reviewing, should be required to reverse
the process, and then called on for principles
and asked to illustrate them.   The aim of the

teacher should be, after awakening interest, not
simply to teach some few facts to which economic principles apply, but to try to drive
home a few fundamental truths, and exercise the
pupil, as far as time and skill allow, in tracing
their operation in facts. For economic facts
are constantly shifting, while principles do not.
A boy taught how properly to view one set
of facts about paper money will go all right as
long as the conditions remain exactly the same,
but when they change he is very badly off for
guidance. In elementary teaching, therefore,
the teacher should aim at giving a clear comprehension of simple principles, and at offering
materials for practice in applying these principles. Much, consequently, which has been said
in regard to more mature students will be
equally applicable to the teaching of young
boys.

In this brief and inadequate way I have at-
tempted to suggest from my own experience
what may enable others to avoid difficulties, and
possibly to aid in a more rational method of
teaching political economy. It is scarcely more

probable that what I have said is all new than that others should agree with me throughout in what I have advanced ; nor is it unlikely that other teachers may have many other suggestions to make in addition to mine. If my efforts may call them out and aid in better methods of teaching, I shall be amply repaid.

THE END.

275 P
275 O

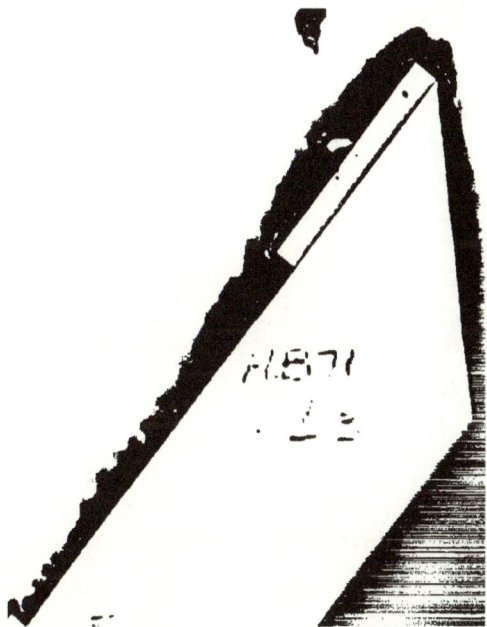

www.ingramcontent.com/pod-product-compliance
Lightning Source LLC
Chambersburg PA
CBHW020552270326
41927CB00006B/810